Negotiating International Commercial Contracts: Practical Exercises

Negotiating International Commercial Contracts: Practical Exercises

Gustavo Moser
Michael McIlwrath

international publishing

Published, sold and distributed by Eleven International Publishing
P.O. Box 85576
2508 CG The Hague
The Netherlands
Tel.: +31 70 33 070 33
Fax: +31 70 33 070 30
e-mail: sales@elevenpub.nl
www.elevenpub.com

Sold and distributed in USA and Canada
Independent Publishers Group
814 N. Franklin Street
Chicago, IL 60610, USA
Order Placement: +1 800 888 4741
Fax: +1 312 337 5985
orders@ipgbook.com
www.ipgbook.com

Eleven International Publishing is an imprint of Boom uitgevers Den Haag.

ISBN 978-94-9094-709-5
NUR 822

© 2021 Gustavo Moser and Michael McIlwrath | Eleven International Publishing

This publication is protected by international copyright law.
All rights reserved. No part of this publication may be reproduced, stored in a retrieval system, or transmitted in any form or by any means, electronic, mechanical, photocopying, recording or otherwise, without the prior permission of the publisher.

Printed in the Netherlands

Introduction

The world of international commerce is as broad in the products and services sold as it is in the range of contracting terms and conditions chosen by the parties. The international commercial lawyer must contend not only with the plain language of the contractual terms being agreed, but the legal effect this 'plain language' will have depending on the law that will govern their interpretation and the arbitrators or judges who will be called to interpret the contract and apply that law in the event of any disputes.

The range of options may seem perplexing or even overwhelming for a lawyer trained to negotiate contracts that will be decided in their domestic courts and applying, naturally, domestic law. Not surprisingly, the approach most frequently taken by many lawyers who find themselves in an international commercial negotiation is not to look for the best possible options for the contract but to try to impose what is most familiar and predictable to them, i.e. their domestic law and courts.[1]

Unless their practice regularly includes resolving international disputes in addition to drafting contracts, even experienced commercial lawyers may not fully appreciate the effect a different law or dispute resolution process may have on the ability to enforce the various terms of the agreement.

The Give-and-Take of International Contract Negotiations vs. 'Drafting' Whatever One Wishes

A lawyer's ability to *negotiate* the terms of an international commercial contract is a key skill that is frequently overlooked or undervalued. Materials tend to focus instead on 'drafting' international contracts. Conferences, for example, frequently include a session on how to 'draft' an arbitration clause, and the term figures

---

1 Empirical studies suggest an overall appreciation of familiarity with respect to the proposed governing contract law: contracting parties often indicate familiarity with the applicable legal system and the cost of becoming accustomed to a 'foreign law' as their chief concerns while choosing to opt in or opt out of a given law or set of rules. See G. Moser, *Rethinking Choice of Law in Cross-Border Sales*, Eleven International Publishing, The Hague, 2018, pp. 1-92.

prominently in the title of many books and articles. While knowing how to write legal concepts is especially helpful for international lawyers, the term tends to invoke an image of a lawyer sitting comfortably behind a desk writing out the exact words that will be included in the parties' contract.

In reality, lawyers participating in an international contract negotiation will often engage in fiery debate over the choice of a particular law or method of dispute resolution, among other terms. When these occasions arise, lawyers must assess whether they can (a) impose on, or persuade, the other side to accept something they do not want; (b) propose a different term as a compromise; (c) accept a potentially defective clause; or (d) walk away from the deal. Behind all of this, there will be pressure from the client (or senior management, in the case of the in-house lawyer), all of whom will be interested in getting the deal done instead of discussing terms.

International contract negotiations always present lawyers with opportunities to propose choices that will enhance their client's objectives, and they can greatly enhance their ability to do this if they are not wedded to the familiar. Of course, if neither side has the information or authority to propose or accept changes, the negotiation may be reduced to a game of each side standing its ground and betting the other will concede. By contrast, the prepared negotiator, who is not encountering the issue for the first time, will be in a position to generate options that may satisfy the interests of both sides or at least will be able to advise whether a perceived risk is genuine and/or acceptable to the party.

International Contracts Are Different from Those between Purely Domestic Parties Mainly Because of Choice of Law and Dispute Resolution Clauses

While this book discusses many different contract terms, its principal focus is on two terms that most distinguish international contracts from those negotiated by parties from the same country and who are applying their own domestic law. The first is the choice of the substantive law to govern the contract (or the failure to choose a law), which will often be a law that is foreign to at least one of the parties and which will affect the significance of the contract's terms *in theory*. The second is the method and place of dispute resolution (or the failure to specify this), which will affect the enforceability of the contract's terms *in practice*.

A Word about the Practice Exercises

The practice format of this book is intended to build proficiency in negotiating a range of issues as you progress through the chapters. These exercises can be performed either alone or in groups. The Appendix contains 'suggested answers' rather than absolute right or wrong solutions.

These guidelines are not exhaustive and are intended to help guide the reader towards the sort of thoughtful approach that will help them negotiate in similar situations and make commercially sensible decisions to avoid being caught by the 'all-too-familiar' approach. They are all topics that can appear (or have appeared!) in real-life situations. In the end, the goal is to negotiate and write international contracts that will not disappoint a party's expectations on those occasions when they must be enforced in further negotiations, or in mediation, or court, or in arbitration.

Table of Contents

Chapter 1 Escaping the Trap of the Familiar in International Contract Negotiations   11
1.1   Every International Commercial Negotiator's Starting Point: Getting Comfortable with Unfamiliar Concepts   11
1.2   And Now the Choice of Law   14

Chapter 2 Negotiating Choice of Law Clauses   21
2.1   Introduction   21
2.2   Differences in How Courts and Arbitrators May Approach 'Foreign Law'   27
2.3   How the CISG Addresses Choice of Law Issues   29

Chapter 3 Negotiating Methods of Dispute Resolution   41
3.1   The Default Rule: Suing the Defendant in the Courts of Their Home Location   42
3.2   The Effect of the Hague Convention on the Choice of Courts   43
3.3   Why a Party May Prefer to Designate the Courts   43
3.4   Considerations When Proposing or Accepting Courts as the Forum   44
       3.4.1   Alternatives to the Courts: Mediation and Arbitration Clauses   49
3.5   The Benefits of Neutrality, Efficiency and Enforceability of Mediation and Arbitration in International Commercial Contracts   50
       3.5.1   Other Reasons Parties Specify Mediation in Their International Contracts   51
       3.5.2   Other Reasons Parties Specify Arbitration in Their International Contracts   52
       3.5.3   The Elements of an Arbitration Clause   52
       3.5.4   The Agreement to Submit Disputes to Arbitration   53
3.6   Emergency or Interim Measures of Protection   54
3.7   The Seat or Place of Arbitration   55
3.8   Big Cities vs. Small Cities   56
3.9   Institutional vs. *Ad Hoc* Arbitration   56

3.10	Choosing among Different Arbitration Institutions	57
3.11	Arbitration vs. Courts: Different Ways of Approaching the Law	60
3.12	Arbitration vs. Courts: Offensive vs. Defensive Strategies	60
3.13	Agreements to Mediate before Arbitration or Court Litigation	62
3.14	Further Practice in Dispute Resolution	63

Chapter 4 Defective Choice of Law and Dispute Resolution Clauses – Prevention and Management of Potential Risks   67

Chapter 5 Putting It All Together   81
5.1	Group Negotiation and Discussion	81
5.2	How Choice of Law and Dispute Resolution Can Alter Certain Contractual Terms	85
5.3	Contractual Limitation of Liability and Choice of Law and Forum	87

Appendix   Guidelines to the Exercises   93

About the Authors   121

Chapter 1 Escaping the Trap of the Familiar in International Contract Negotiations

> **Learning Objectives:**
> – Enhance the reader's ability to anticipate legal and business risks and minimize potential pitfalls
> – Assist the reader to make commercially sensible decisions to avoid being caught up by the 'all-too-familiar' approach

1.1 Every International Commercial Negotiator's Starting Point: Getting Comfortable with Unfamiliar Concepts

Most lawyers receive their legal education and subsequent training and experience with only one legal system, and they grow increasingly accustomed to advising clients on optimal solutions that they have learned. At some point, the day arrives when they must advise their client on an international commercial contract. How hidebound will they remain to their training in their own national system when other legal principles could be introduced, potentially equal to or in some cases worse, and in others superior to, those with which they are most familiar?
Consider a lawyer in New York who represents a New York seller of goods to a Singaporean buyer with all of its revenues and assets in Singapore and who is in turn represented by a Singaporean lawyer. The New York seller has told their lawyer that their greatest concern is the ability to enforce their right to payment since the Singaporean buyer is unwilling to agree to advance payments. Further, the Singaporean company has no assets in New York or anywhere else in the United States and is unable or unwilling to provide any security for the contract's payment obligations, for example, through a bank letter of credit. Thus, if the buyer defaults, the only way for the seller to be paid will be through a legal action.
This New York lawyer has experience only with contract negotiations and litigation in the United States. She is considering different options for choice of law and

dispute resolution in this negotiation. Which of the options below do you think she is most likely to insist upon? And which do you think will most likely protect her client's entitlement to payment?
a.   Silence on the questions of governing law or dispute resolution.
b.   The contract would be governed by New York law, with any disputes to be resolved by litigation in the courts of New York.
c.   The contract would be governed by English law and disputes to be settled by international arbitration, with London as the seat.
d.   The contract would be governed by Singaporean law, with any litigation in the courts of Singapore, the buyer's country.

You probably guessed she will insist on (b), because that is what she is most familiar with. In fact, the available data suggests you would be correct; 'familiar' is the most common choice among lawyers.[2]
But the second question is whether this is the best option.
Most lawyers will likely reject option (a), and for good reason. For an international commercial contract, silence on choice of law and dispute resolution injects a good deal of uncertainty. It will rarely be the preferred option of a competent or experienced lawyer.
Option (b), however, does not appear to be optimal for the seller. The New York lawyer may feel she can confidently endorse her home state's law and courts as a means to provide a fair dispute resolution process. But a fair process will be meaningless to her client if the result does not lead to a payment. With no payment security and a buyer that has no assets in the United States, our New York lawyer risks recommending to her client to accept contract terms that will lead to victory in name only, since a US court judgment may have limited or little authority in the countries where the buyer has assets.
While a multi-lateral treaty to recognize and enforce the foreign court judgments of certain countries is in the early stages of adoption and its success remains to be seen,[3] for now parties seeking cross-border enforcement have only one of two avenues to pursue:
–   Identify whether a *bilateral* treaty exists between both countries for enforcing each other's court judgments and seek to enforce the judgment of the foreign country under the terms of the treaty. Even when such a bilateral treaty exists,

---

2   G. Moser, *supra* note 1, pp. 33-92.
3   The Hague Conference of Private International Law concluded the Convention on the Recognition and Enforcement of Foreign Judgments in Civil or Commercial Matters on 2 July 2019 (*the Judgments Convention*). The Judgments Convention provides for the mutual enforcement of court judgments not limited to exclusive jurisdiction clauses, the full text of which is available here: www.hcch.net/en/projects/legislative-projects/judgments. On the date of publication, there were no published instances of the courts of any country having relied upon the Judgments Convention to order the enforcement of a foreign court's judgment.

CHAPTER 1 ESCAPING THE TRAP OF THE FAMILIAR IN INTERNATIONAL CONTRACT NEGOTIATIONS

    however, the enforcing courts may be reluctant to enforce a 'judgment' rendered by a foreign court of first instance if an appeal has been lodged and remains pending.[4]

– In the absence of a treaty, the judgment creditor must initiate enforcement proceedings in the country of the judgment debtor's assets under court principles of comity, i.e. the mechanisms by which a court will ensure itself that adequate due process has been applied to the rendering of the judgment. Of course, the court will not apply due process as it is known at the place of judgment, but that with which the court itself is most familiar, i.e. Singapore procedure. This gives the judgment debtor another bite at the apple. In addition, we face the same problem with enforcement treaties: the judgment creditor may not be able to initiate enforcement until all appeals have been exhausted.

Accordingly, the option that is most familiar to the seller's lawyer may well be the least optimal to achieve her client's main objective.

Option (c), international arbitration in London, may be a logical choice, and it is not a bad one. It is usually much easier to enforce an international arbitration award because of the existence of a multilateral treaty, the 1958 United Nations Convention on the Recognition and Enforcement of Foreign Arbitral Awards (also called "the New York Convention"[5]), discussed in more detail in Chapter 3.[6] Under the New York Convention, signatory states agree to treat arbitration award rendered in another signatory state as enforceable as if they were a judgment of the court of first instance.[7] Both the United Kingdom and Singapore are signatories to the New York Convention. Thus, if a creditor can immediately enforce a domestic court judgment in Singapore, then they can also enforce an arbitration award rendered in London.

While there are some specified exceptions to enforcement, such as violation of public policy or fraud, foreign arbitral awards are typically given effect under the New York Convention. Also, Singapore is widely regarded as an 'arbitration-friendly' country.

But let us consider the last option, (d), especially if the seller's only or main concern is the ability to sue promptly for payment. Thus, the option that will be

---

4   For example, even within the framework of European regulations, European courts may suspend enforcement when an appeal has been lodged in the judgment's country of origin. A. Pertoldi & G. Horlock, 'Conditions for Recognition and Enforcement of Foreign Judgments in the United Kingdom', available at www.lexology.com/library/detail.aspx?g=e7614f91-c3b8-4d7b-9b5e-82634f47fcac.

5   The text of the 1958 New York Convention is available at www.uncitral.org/pdf/english/texts/arbitration/NY-conv/New-York-Convention-E.pdf.

6   *See* Chapter 3, para. 3.5 and 3.11.

7   A worldwide database of decisions under the 1958 New York Convention is available at http://newyorkconvention1958.org.

the least familiar to the New York lawyer, litigation in the courts of the buyer, may be the best method for her to achieve her client's key objective.[8]

It is also important for her to know (or be able to find out), however, that Singapore courts have a reputation for being relatively reliable and efficient, and may even be faster (and certainly not slower) than an international arbitration followed by the need to initiate recognition and enforcement proceedings in Singapore (if the debtor does not voluntarily and promptly pay).

At this point, the reader may be worried that each dispute resolution or choice of law decision requires encyclopaedic knowledge of the court practices of various countries. Not at all.

In this particular example, a lawyer who simply questions whether their domestic dispute resolution is the best way to achieve the client's objective will already be more likely to achieve the client's objectives than one who simply insists on what they are most familiar with instead. It is a good starting point in international commercial negotiations to question what is most familiar and understand that it may not be optimal. This is especially so if negotiating to obtain the 'home advantage' also requires the negotiator to compromise on other important terms of the contract, such as price and delivery.

1.2   And Now the Choice of Law

Lawyers regularly negotiate whether to agree that a judge or arbitrator should decide any disputes under the contract, where they should be decided and under what rules, as well as what substantive law should apply. International commercial lawyers learn to use these as interconnected tools where, for example, changing the governing law may affect whether a judge or arbitrator would be best suited to decide any disputes, rather than as separate and independent from each other.

Going back to our New York-Singapore example above, suppose our lawyer recognizes that submitting a claim in the courts of Singapore would be the quickest and most reliable route to obtaining payment if the buyer defaults on their obligations. And let us suppose further that the New York lawyer does what most lawyers are inclined to do, which is to insist that the contract be governed by the laws of her home jurisdiction, New York, because she knows it and is qualified to advise the client on it.

Can a Singaporean judge apply New York law? Of course. But *how* would a Singaporean judge likely apply it? Judges, too, tend to prefer what is most familiar. Rarely are judges trained in applying foreign law, and even when they are, they typically will have little experience doing so. It should seem obvious that a New York lawyer should not reasonably expect a judge in Singapore to apply domestic New York law the same way it would be applied by a judge sitting in New York. And yet this compromise solution is occasionally the result of international

---

[8]   M. McIlwrath & J. Savage, *International Arbitration & Mediation: A Practical Guide*, Kluwer Law International, Alphen aan den Rijn, 2010, p. 17.

contract negotiations, potentially to the disappointment of both sides to the contract when they later try to enforce the contract according to their expectations. Yet our New York lawyer may yet have more in her bag of tricks that will make her feel more comfortable in advising her client on a contract that will be governed by a foreign law on which she is not qualified. That is, what is 'New York law' or 'Singapore law' in this context? By familiarizing herself with the 1980 United Nations Convention on Contracts for the International Sale of Goods (CISG[9]), she will know that both Singapore and the United States have ratified the CISG.[10] Since her client is selling goods from New York to a buyer in Singapore, the CISG will apply to her contract.

Therefore, by agreeing that the contract will be governed by 'Singapore law', she is really accepting 'Singapore's law of international sales'. Since that is Singapore's implementation of the CISG, it will be similar to New York's law of international sales, which is also an implementation of the CISG.

Once a country formally accedes to the CISG,[11] and 94 have at the date of this publication,[12] the CISG becomes incorporated into its legal system and is "national law"[13] with respect to contracts for the international sales of goods with parties in other states that have accepted the CISG. Thus, the lawyer may be able to advise her client that, while counter-intuitive, agreeing to resolve disputes in Singapore courts applying the law of Singapore is even more reliable than a compromise that combines Singapore court with New York governing law.

In some cases, however, lawyers overlook this opportunity because they do not appreciate the relationship that choice of law will have on the enforcement of the contract. Indeed, empirical studies on choice of law in international contracts indicate that lawyers often add boilerplate (standard) language from other

---

9 The text of the CISG is available at www.cisg.law.pace.edu/cisg/text/treaty.html.
10 The list of CISG contracting states is available at https://uncitral.un.org/en/texts/salegoods/conventions/sale_of_goods/cisg/status
11 In this sense, *see* Art. 100 of the CISG:
   Art. 100
   (1) This Convention applies to the formation of a contract only when the proposal for concluding the contract is made on or after the date when the Convention enters into force in respect of the Contracting States referred to in subparagraph (1)(a) or the Contracting State referred to in subparagraph (1)(b) of article 1.
   (2) This Convention applies only to contracts concluded on or after the date when the Convention enters into force in respect of the Contracting States referred to in subparagraph (1)(a) or the Contracting State referred to in subparagraph (1)(b) of article 1.
12 *See supra* note 9.
13 This is addressed in Chapter 2, *infra*, para. 2.1, *see also* G. Moser, *supra* note 1, p. 58; and L.G. Meira Moser, 'CISG in Brazilian Courts: A Promising Start – Case Commentary on Inversiones Metalmecánicas I.C.A. v. Voges Metalurgia Ltd.', *Internationales Handelsrecht*, Vol. 16, Issue 4, 2016, pp. 133-136.

CHAPTER 1 ESCAPING THE TRAP OF THE FAMILIAR IN INTERNATIONAL CONTRACT NEGOTIATIONS

documents to exclude the application of the CISG, such as "this contract shall be governed by the laws of Singapore to the exclusion of the CISG".[14] Is it a good idea to exclude the legal effect of a widely adopted international treaty because a lawyer is unfamiliar with them? As we will see in Chapter 2,[15] probably not.

Exercises: Basic

This section sets out several exercises based on commonly discussed points in international commercial contract negotiations. They are aimed at developing confidence in accepting 'unfamiliar' choices of law and dispute resolution.

Exercise 1.1: Is home court better?
Amelie and Vishal are in-house lawyers for companies headquartered in France and India, respectively. They are negotiating a stock purchase agreement (SPA) by which Amelie's company will acquire a subsidiary of Vishal's company in India. All of the terms have been agreed except for choice of law and a forum for dispute resolution. Please assess the situations below:

A. Dispute forum: Amelie has initiated this negotiation by proposing that any disputes under the acquisition agreement should be resolved in the courts of Paris, which is the acquiring company's principal place of business. Leaving aside considerations of whether French courts are regarded as independent and efficient, what sort of questions do you think Amelie and Vishal should consider before agreeing with Amelie's proposal?

B. Governing law: Vishal's boss, the General Counsel (GC), prefers all of the company's contracts to be governed by Indian law. He is an experienced Indian lawyer and feels comfortable about his domestic laws. But this is an international contract, and the GC recognizes that the buyer is unlikely to accept Indian law, and he does not want this to become a distracting issue in the negotiations. He has asked Vishal to recommend the best governing law for this international M&A deal. Which of these is the *first* issue Vishal should consider before making a proposal to his GC, and why?

  a. Whether English or Singapore law would be good alternatives because they are both common law systems that share much with Indian law;
  b. Whether the law is from a country with a stable and highly regarded legal system;
  c. What disputes are likely to arise under this M&A contract and which laws will be most advantageous should one of those disputes arise.

---

14 G. Moser, *supra* note 1, pp. 1-92. For a complete analysis of the main drivers that often lead contracting parties to exclude the CISG, *see* pp. 33-92. For a discussion on the level of rationality of these choices, and the factors and underlying motives that influence these decisions, *see* G. Moser, *supra* note 1, pp. 93-116.
15 *See* Chapter 2 *infra*, para. 2.1.

CHAPTER 1 ESCAPING THE TRAP OF THE FAMILIAR IN INTERNATIONAL CONTRACT NEGOTIATIONS

Exercise 1.2: Small city problems
After a day of negotiations, Amelie and Vishal have agreed that the contract's dispute resolution procedure will be arbitration, but they have not agreed on the seat of the arbitration. Amelie has proposed Grenoble, a small French town in the Alps where her client's company has its headquarters. The town has a population of 160,000 and has its own courthouse with a small pool of judges who handle commercial litigation as well as labour, family, tax, administrative and environmental disputes. Which of the following might present a problem in procedure for setting up the arbitration or enforcing any award, even for Amelie's own client, if Grenoble is accepted as the seat?
a. A small town in the Alps will not be convenient for hearings, for the arbitrators, or even Amelie and her colleagues as lawyers who will be coming from other parts of France.
b. The judges are not likely to have much experience with international arbitration, and this could be a problem if either of the parties challenges the award (which is the jurisdiction of the courts at the legal seat of the arbitration).
c. If there is any arbitration hearing in the winter, the arbitrators could get hurt while skiing and this could cause the proceedings to be delayed.

Exercise 1.3: Seat connection needed?
Continuing to negotiate, Amelie and Vishal have narrowed the choice of seat of arbitration to either Paris or London. Amelie insists on Paris because, she says, neither party has any connection with London or the United Kingdom, and therefore an arbitration in London risks being invalid. Vishal insists that the parties can choose any city in the world as the seat of arbitration. Who is right and why?
a. Amelie
b. Vishal
c. Both

Exercise 1.4: Does it matter where international arbitration institutions are located?
After further back-and-forth discussions, Amelie and Vishal have agreed to London as the seat of the arbitration and for the contract to be governed by English law. Their last point of disagreement is the rules of arbitration to adopt. Amelie is insisting on the Rules of Arbitration of the International Chamber of Commerce (ICC), while Vishal demands the LCIA (London Court of International Arbitration). Vishal is adamant that the ICC cannot be designated because it is headquartered in Paris and insists the LCIA should be used because it is headquartered in London, the same as the place of arbitration, and English is the governing law. Amelie disagrees and says the ICC rules can apply to an arbitration in London, just as the LCIA rules could apply to an arbitration seated in Paris. Who is right and why?

17

a. Amelie
b. Vishal
c. Both

Notes

CHAPTER 1 ESCAPING THE TRAP OF THE FAMILIAR IN INTERNATIONAL CONTRACT NEGOTIATIONS

Chapter 2 Negotiating Choice of Law Clauses

> **Learning Objectives:**
> - Choice of law 'in the abstract'
> - What happens if the parties do not choose a law to govern their contract
> - Domestic law vs. 'foreign law'
> - Domestic courts vs. international arbitration: a different mindset towards the application of 'foreign law'
> - The United Nations Convention on Contracts for the International Sale of Goods (CISG)

2.1 Introduction

In contract negotiations, a party invariably encounters situations in which its own optimal action contrasts with what the other party desires. The most basic example, of course, is that of a buyer wishing to pay the lowest possible amount and the seller wishing to receive as much as possible. The conflicts between party positions extend throughout their contractual arrangements, regardless of whether they are embodied in the terms they negotiate or those on which they remain silent.

The legal regulation of contracts involving parties coming from different legal systems imposes additional difficulties that are both subjective and objective.

Subjectively, parties will have formed their own views of the rules of private international law, which may be based on a combination of cultural and geographical factors. These perceptions may interfere with the success of a deal from the perspective of one or both parties to an international commercial agreement.[16] Significantly, parties are often unwilling to subject themselves to the law of the counterparty.[17] The reasons include the counterparty's perception vs.

---

16 G. Moser, *supra* note 1, p. 118.
17 As C. Fountoulakis explains, the parties are familiar with their own law and are convinced that they will save considerable costs in not being required to investigate the

their actual knowledge of the other's law,[18] what they may see as seller-/buyer-friendly national laws or a fear of laws simply being biased towards nationals of that country.[19] And one party's fear of the other's law will often be reciprocated by the perceptions held by the counterparty.

Objectively, there will often be laws that offer a genuinely better legal framework for a party than others, often better than the one that the party prefers as a result of the subjective factors that influence its preferences. Objective factors can include substantive differences among legal regimes and whether and how certain contract terms will be enforced; restrictions that may affect one or both parties' autonomy where the choice of law touches upon mandatory provisions; and unknown, confusing or hermetic conflict of law rules.[20]

How, therefore, should a party approach the issue of the choice of law to govern an international commercial contract, assuming that both parties have some degree of manoeuvrability in their negotiation of this point?[21]

As previously discussed, contracting parties will likely prefer the law with which they are most familiar, because it gives them a degree of certainty and predictability. In cross-border transactions, where a party may choose among a myriad of laws, a party's comfort in having its own law may clash with the law that may be more efficient or optimal with regard to its interests in the contract.[22]

There is certainly no one-size-fits-all "best law" for all international commercial agreements, but in choosing among different options, parties should consider, at a minimum, including accessibility[23] (parties, counsel and arbitrators can examine it

---

    intricacies of foreign law. Moreover, if they have their own law applied, they do not have to consult external experts but rather can rely on their usual, well-acquainted legal advisors. The author goes further and states that the parties to an international contract will strive towards an application of their own law, even if that law is less suitable for the transaction at hand than the other law might be. See C. Fountoulakis, 'The Parties' Choice of "Neutral Law" in International Sales Contracts', *European Journal of Law Reform*, Vol. VII, Issue 3/4, 2005, pp. 303-329, p. 304.

18 L.G. Meira Moser, 'Parties' Preferences in International Sales Contracts: An Empirical Analysis of the Choice of Law', *Uniform Law Review*, Vol. 20, Issue 1, 2015, pp. 19-55, p. 32.

19 G. Moser, *supra* note 1, p. 131.

20 *Id.*, p. 118.

21 Although we are addressing situations where the parties are able to negotiate the law that will govern their contract, the considerations in this chapter will also be useful for parties to assess situations in which the other party (usually the customer or party with economic leverage) seeks to impose a particular law and there is no ability to negotiate, only 'take it or leave it'.

22 For a discussion on efficiency and law and its intersection with economics, please *see* G. Moser, *supra* note 1, pp. 120-122.

23 Professor Julian Lew QC observes that "in international arbitration, as with the absence of the forum's conflict of law rules, there are no rules expressed as to how a

and ascertain its merits with a minimum of difficulty), predictability (the legal system on which the law relies should be stable and not likely to radically alter its foundational principles), the effect given to the parties' agreement and the interpretation of key terms, and public policy.[24]

Obviously, in contract negotiation and drafting, one should reflect on the consequences if the contract subsequently must be enforced against a breaching party, both with respect to the contract's specific terms and points where it is silent. In an ideal world, contracts would have few elements and would leave the indeterminacies to be interpreted and decided by an adjudicator, i.e. a judge or arbitrator. Even in such cases, however, a judge or arbitrator will not be able to enforce the contract without a particular law to refer that 'maps' what the parties intended to achieve.[25]

For example, parties may or may not choose a particular law or rules in order to (i) prevent the application of less 'credible' laws or rules and parties' benefitting from a more acceptable legal framework; (ii) avoid a particular law or rules so as to escape the application of other laws (for various reasons, including the lack of trust in that law's or rules' application by state court judges); or (iii) ensure that a given legal framework concerning which the parties have bargained would apply fully.[26]

---

tribunal should determine the content to the relevant law and the specific rules it should apply. However, the expectation is that a tribunal will correctly apply the substantive rules to issues presented by the facts in each case. The need to ascertain the content of the applicable law is an essential task of the international arbitral tribunal." See J. D. M. Lew QC, 'Iura Novit Curia and Due Process', *Queen Mary School of Law Legal Studies Research Paper No. 72/2010*, 2011, p. 2, available at https://ssrn.com/abstract=1733531.

24 See J.B. Tieder, 'Factors to Consider in the Choice of Procedural and Substantive Law in International Arbitration', *Journal of International Arbitration*, Vol. 20, Issue 4, 2003, p. 405; M. Blessing, 'Choice of Substantive Law in International Arbitration', *Journal of International Arbitration*, Vol. 14, Issue 2, 1997; O. Lando, 'The Law Applicable to the Merits of the Dispute', *Kluwer Law International*, Vol. 2, Issue 2, 1986, pp. 104-115; and J.D.M. Lew QC, 'The Law Applicable to the Form and Substance of the Arbitration Clause', *in* Albert Jan van den Berg (Ed.), *Improving the Efficiency of Arbitration Agreements and Awards: 40 Years of Application of the New York Convention*, ICCA Congress Series, Volume 9, Kluwer Law International, Alphen aan den Rijn, 1999, pp. 114-145.

25 A. Schwartz & R.E. Scott, 'Contract Theory and the Limits of Contract Law', *Yale Law Journal*, Vol. 113, 2003, pp. 540-596, p. 547.

26 G. Moser, 'Choice of Law, Brexit and the "Ice Cream Flavour" Dilemma', *Kluwer Arbitration Blog*, 14 November 2018, available at http://arbitrationblog.kluwerarbitration.com/2018/11/14/choice-of-law-brexit-arbitration-and-the-ice-cream-flavour-dilemma/.

Consider for example a negotiation of a sale of granulated iron ore between an English buyer and a seller in Saudi Arabia. English and Saudi parties will both be tempted to propose their domestic laws,[27] for reasons discussed above.

Both parties will likely desire the law applicable to their contract to be readily accessible and intelligible to the parties, their counsel and the decision-makers. Predictability is a vital feature that parties desire; they wish to avoid unpleasant surprises. But while they may perceive their own law to be perfectly suited to the contract, the other party may not share this perception.

Further, national laws are typically not written in 'black-and-white'; there are always shades involved, which the parties' lawyers may not be aware of until they find themselves in a situation where they are forced to access that law for a contract dispute. And the reality is that, domestic laws actually are often short-sighted, drafted to govern domestic affairs[28] and seldom, if ever, fit in a large international context.

In order to avoid concerns regarding the applicable law,[29] uniform laws, such as the United Nations Convention on Contracts for the International Sale of Goods (CISG),[30] provide default provisions on key contractual aspects.[31] The advantage of

---

27 'Home law' is typically associated with 'familiarity' and generally represents one of the 'go to' options of the parties in decision-making processes. *See* more G. Moser, *supra* note 1, pp. 1-92. *A contrario sensu*, *see* analysis of cognitive biases, including 'familiarity', which explains how decisions based upon 'familiarity' may blur or influence this process negatively. *See*, in this sense, G. Moser, *supra* note 1, pp. 93-116.

28 M. Blessing, *supra* note 24, pp. 39-66, p. 41.

29 For further reference on this context, see E. Muñoz & L.G. Meira Moser, '*Brazil's Adhesion to the CISG* – Consequences for Trade in China and Latin-America', *in* I. Schwenzer & L. Spagnolo (Eds.), *Globalization versus Regionalization – 4th Annual MAA Schlechtriem CISG Conference*, Eleven International Publishing, The Hague, 2013, pp. 79-96.

30 To promote uniformity in this area of law, the CISG was created under the auspices of the United Nations Commission on International Trade Law (UNCITRAL), the United Nations body responsible for drafting model laws for the standardization and/or harmonization of international trade. *See 1980-United Nations Convention on Contracts for the International Sale of Goods*, United Nations Commission on International Trade Law, available at www.uncitral.org/uncitral/uncitral_texts/sale_goods/1980CISG.html. The CISG is divided into four parts: a general part on definitions, sphere of application and rules of construction (Arts. 1-13); a second part on contract formation (Arts. 14-24); a third part on general provisions and rights and obligations of the parties to an international sales contract (Arts. 25-88); and a final part on how states may formally adopt the CISG, including reservations (Arts. 89-101). The full text of the CISG is available at www.cisg.law.pace.edu/cisg/text/treaty.html.

31 As L.A. Dimatteo & D. Ostas argue, employing the common core and better rules approaches resulted in an interesting amalgam of common and civil law rules.

uniform laws is that they are tailored to tackle some of the main legal risks that are associated with the choice of a governing law.[32] The CISG itself deals with the cross-border sale of goods.

The CISG operates by means of uniform rules, which notably cover the formation (and burden of proof) of the contract, the interpretation of the parties' previous (and current) dealings and conduct, warranties for defects and other obligations of the seller, in addition to the consequences arising from breach of the relationship, default, termination of contract and damages.[33]

Another advantage of using uniform contract laws is that they are neutral. Neither party is directly associated or identified with them and, therefore, neither has a particular advantage when proposing or applying it.[34]

Parties whose states have adopted uniform laws may find it both easier and less risky to engage in international commercial transactions because there will be less uncertainty when applying these regimes.[35] The potential battle over the choice of governing law may be considerably reduced and the applicable law will not be

---

The CISG consists of rules that can be characterized as follows: (1) rules consistent with both common and civil law legal traditions, (2) rules that recognize the superiority of a given common or civil-law rule – at least for the sake of transborder transactions, (3) rules that are fabricated to be national-system neutral, (4) rules that abdicate to national law by expressly refusing to cover certain topics and (5) rules that fit in one of the first three categories but are subject to modification by the CISG's preference for original or autonomous interpretation of its rules (pp. 376-377). See L.A. Dimatteo & D. Ostas, 'Comparative Efficiency in International Sales Law', *American University International Law Journal*, Vol. 26, Issue 2, 2011, pp. 371-439.

32 *See*, in this sense, F. de Ly remarking cross-cultural, transaction costs and contract management as advantages of the CISG 'The Relevance of the Vienna Convention for International Sales Contracts – Should We Stop Contracting It Out?', *Business Law International*, Issue 3, 2003, pp. 241-249, pp. 241, 246.

33 G. Moser, *supra* note 1, p. 174.

34 C. Fountoulakis, *supra* note 17, p. 314; L.G. Meira Moser, *supra* note 18, p. 28.

35 The CISG extracts models of civil law and common-law elements capable of harmonizing trade between countries of different legal traditions. *See* C. Samson, 'L'harmonisation du droit de la vente internationale de merchandises entre pays de droit civil et pays de common law', *Contemporary Law: Canadian Reports to the 1990 International Congress of Comparative Law*, 1990, pp. 100-125; B. Goldman, 'Frontières du droit et lex mercatoria', *Archives de philosophie du droit*, Vol. 9, 1964, p. 177 *et seq*; E. Gaillard, 'Trente ans de lex mercatoria. Pour une application sélective de la méthode des principes généraux du droit', *Journal du Droit International*, No. I, 1995, pp. 5-30; B. Oppetit, 'La notion de source du droit et le droit du commerce international', *Archives de philosophie du droit*, Vol. 27, 1982, pp. 43-53; B. Oppetit, 'Autour du contrat international', *Droits*, Vol. 12, 1990, pp. 107-115; P. Schlechriem & C. Witz, *Convention de Vienne sur les Contrats de Vente Internationale de Marchandises*, Dalloz, Paris, 2008; I. Schwenzer (Ed.), *Schlechtriem & Schwenzer*,

'foreign' to any of the parties, reducing the costs of learning or responding to a world of possible laws to choose from in each contract negotiation.[36]

How does a court judge apply the law to a given international contract (a) when the parties have not specified a particular law and (b) when they have done so?[37]

As a practical matter, courts faced with determining the law applicable to an international dispute face a range of issues, not the least of which is whether the disputed issue is one over which the parties have the freedom to choose from. Take, for example, an Australian couple who, after being married in Australia, move to France where they live with their children for many years and then file for divorce in Paris. The French court hearing the case may have no difficulty applying Australian law to the separation of the assets acquired by the couple before and during their marriage. But when it comes to the determination of whether one or another parent is fit to have custody of the children and other matters related to their well-being, the French court will look to the French laws regarding the rights of family.

This is because marriage is a matter of contract, and the marriage agreement was stipulated in Australia. But the court must consider that children are obviously not assets arising from the couple's marriage; the court must recognize they are human beings with their own rights and whose well-being is protected by the laws of the country where they reside.

With regard to purely commercial matters that do not involve such delicate questions as the well-being of children, courts will still face issues of whether the applicable law is one that is attached to a particular place.

As a matter of technique, the task of determining the applicable law is a twofold process. It requires the judge to firstly undertake a 'qualification' of the legal relationship and then identify the 'connection' to a given legal system. If we translate this into an equation, we would have: qualification + connection = applicable law.

In qualifying, the court judge classifies the facts into legal categories, such as a property right or personal right, a fact, an act, a legal transaction, etc. If the result of the classification is a contract, the court judge must determine its legal nature: administrative, commercial, consumer, etc. The classification could be based on the *lex fori*, *lex loci celebrationis* rule, *locus regit actum*, *lex causae*, *lex loci protectionis* etc.[38]

After qualifying the fact, it will be necessary to connect it to a given legal system. For this, there are rules of private international law which will connect the fact to legal systems. Thus, in the case of personal status, personal rights will apply; in the

---

Commentary on the United Nations Convention on the International Sale of Goods (CISG), 4th ed., Oxford University Press, Oxford, 2016.

36   G. Cuniberti, 'Is the CISG Benefiting Anybody?', *Vanderbilt Journal of Transnational Law*, Vol. 39, 2006, pp. 1511-1550.
37   L.G. Meira Moser, *supra* note 13.
38   *Id.*, pp. 134-135.

case of property status, the law of the place where the goods are situated; in the case of facts and legal acts, the law of the place of their occurrence, in addition to other connecting factors such as *lex fori, lex loci delicti commissi, lex loci executionis*, etc.

As regards contractual obligations, a national court or domestic arbitral tribunal could find, for example, that its laws provide for the application of "the law of the country in which contractual obligations are established shall apply to qualify and govern such obligations".[39] But what this means in practice is an entirely different matter and may be influenced by the location or orientation of the judge or arbitrator who is called to apply this reasoning in a dispute.

Exercise: Intermediate

> *Exercise 2.1: Whose Law Applies?*
> A seller in Wetar Island (Indonesia) and a buyer in Riyadh (Saudi Arabia) negotiate and conclude by telephone and email exchanges an agreement for the purchase of wood charcoal, which is stored in the seller's warehouse in Dili (East Timor). From there, the goods will be shipped to the port of Al Jasra (Bahrain) where the buyer maintains a warehouse and a number of other businesses. Neither Indonesia nor Saudi Arabia – where the seller and buyer, respectively, have their principal place of business – are signatories to the CISG. In the absence of a law specified by their contract or any international treaty to govern this transaction, what are the potential applicable laws that will be used to interpret the contract in the event of a dispute?
> a. The laws of the Kingdom of Saudi Arabia
> b. The laws of East Timor
> c. The laws of Indonesia
> d. The laws of Bahrain

2.2 Differences in How Courts and Arbitrators May Approach 'Foreign Law'

As the preceding section illustrates, judges face a particular challenge when they are called to apply a law other than their own. They may struggle when the facts of an international commercial transaction point to more than one country as a potential source of law applicable to the contract or a dispute that arises under it. While some may have occasional exposure to foreign laws, domestic judges typically hear local, domestic cases and do not have substantial training in applying the laws of other countries.

In very broad terms, there are two types of arbitrators: domestic and international. Arbitrators in the first category are those who practice mainly arbitrations between parties from the same country. They rarely face disagreements as to which law applies, because they will usually share the same national law as the parties. Domestic arbitrators are often very similar to judges in both how they manage

---

39 *Id.*

cases and how they assess the evidence and legal arguments presented. Fearing that their award will be challenged by a losing party if it does not conform adequately to the national law, their arbitration awards are often indistinguishable from domestic court decisions in their form of drafting.

The second type of arbitrator, which is the greater focus of this book, is the international practitioner. They are likely to be appointed in cases in which the parties are from different countries, and their counsel and the other arbitrators may be from still other countries. There is a reasonable expectation that the arbitrators sitting in an international arbitration should be capable of applying laws that are foreign to their nationality and/or training.

Exercises: Basic

Exercise 2.2: You Be the Judge!
Continuing with the example of the seller in Wetar Island (Indonesia) and the buyer in Saudi Arabia, assume that the buyer defaulted on their payment obligation after claiming the goods were defective. The seller has filed a claim in the courts of Jakarta, Indonesia's capital, where the seller has their principal place of business. You are the judge in Jakarta hearing this dispute. Assume that, as an Indonesian judge, you are confident in your ability to apply Indonesian law and less confident in applying other law. What considerations will you use to determine which law will apply to the contract and this dispute?

Exercise 2.3: Enforcing a Foreign Judgment
Now assume the seller has obtained a favourable judgment from the Jakarta court based on the application of the Indonesian law to the parties' contract. The buyer is refusing to pay the seller, however, and now wishes to enforce it in Saudi Arabia. You are the Saudi judge to whom the case is assigned. If there are no international treaties in place by which Saudi courts must enforce judgments rendered in Indonesia, what grounds might you consider to refuse to enforce the Indonesian court judgment?

Exercise 2.4: Choice of Court without Choice of Law
Continuing with the same contract, assume that it contains a choice of dispute resolution clause that reads as follows: "Article 27.2. Any contractual disputes arising out of this contract shall be decided before the courts of Riyadh", but there is no express choice of law in the contract. If the seller files their claim in Riyadh, is it certain that the Saudi court will apply Saudi law? What arguments might be raised by the parties about the application of different laws?

Exercise: Intermediate

Exercise 2.5: Choice of Court with(out) Choice of Law
Would any of the following change your answer to the exercises above?
  i. The dispute resolution clause reads as follows: "Article 27.2. Any contractual disputes arising out of this contract shall be decided before the courts of Bahrain".
  ii. There was an arbitration clause stating that the arbitrators shall apply the law "most closely connected with the contract performance".
  iii. The contract did not designate a forum for resolving disputes.

2.3 How the CISG Addresses Choice of Law Issues

The CISG is an international treaty that has been ratified by 94 different countries[40] and is product of a compromise[41] obtained from 62 countries that participated at the outset of its discussions.[42] Given the degree of legal diversity among the participants, the only way to harmonize substantive rules of contract law was to compromise. From this, participating states were required to abandon the idea that the CISG rules reflect their own legal system,[43] thereby adopting a conciliatory approach.[44]

If you were to look at the contracts in which the parties chose to exclude the application of the CISG, you would think that the CISG's purpose was to undermine the commercial stability of contracts provided by the designated law. In fact, the purpose of the CISG is the very opposite: to promote international trade of goods by providing a stable and reasonable framework for the parties to enforce

---

40 The list of CISG contracting states is available at https://uncitral.un.org/en/texts/salegoods/conventions/sale_of_goods/cisg/status.
41 As it happens, the process of drafting the CISG has not been welcomed by everyone. Gillete & Scott brought forward a criticism suggesting that "the structure of the ISL [CISG] drafting process would produce a treaty (1) that contained many vague and ambiguous provisions resulting in formal uniformity without substantive uniformity; (2) that allowed nations otherwise bound by CISG provisions to contract out with relative ease; and (3) that would generate divergent interpretations undermining even the initial benefits of formal uniformity", p. 473, C.P. Gillette & R.E. Scott, 'The Political Economy of International Sales Law', *International Review of Law and Economics*, Vol. 25, 2005, pp. 446-486.
42 For a historical recap of the CISG, see C. M. Bianca & M. J. Bonell, *Commentary on the International Sales Law – The 1980 Vienna Sales Convention*, Giuffrè, Milan, 1987, pp. 3-7; and P. Schlechtriem, *Uniform Sales Law, The UN-Convention on Contracts for the International Sale of Goods*, Manzsche Verlags – und Universitatsbuchhandlung, Vienna, 1986, pp. 17-23.
43 G. Moser, *supra* note 1, p. 182.
44 *Id.*, p. 181.

their contracts, consistent with generally accepted commercial principles and the business expectations that arise in international contracting. In addition, the CISG rules were intended and designed to generate efficiency and facilitate trade worldwide. This is proved by the terms of its preamble, which state that the CISG aimed at contributing for "the removal of legal barriers in international trade and promote the development of international trade".[45]

Another aspect to note in the context of the CISG's goal of removing legal barriers is that the CISG rules cannot be associated with any contracting party directly and, therefore, neither party has a particular advantage over its counterparty when proposing or applying the CISG legal framework – the parties are thus considered to be on a *quasi*-same 'level playing field'.[46]

(a) The Choice of the CISG by the Arbitral Tribunal's Own Initiative

In cases of inadvertent or deliberate omission of a choice of law clause in the agreement, the CISG may apply where the parties to the international commercial agreement are both from contracting states to the CISG and their agreement involves the sale of goods.

Article 1 of the CISG outlines the scope of application of the CISG and reads as follows:

> (1) This Convention applies to contracts of sale of goods between parties whose places of business are in different States:
> a) when the States are Contracting States; or
> b) when the rules of private international law lead to the application of the law of a Contracting State.
>
> (2) The fact that the parties have their places of business in different States is to be disregarded whenever this fact does not appear either from the contract or from any dealings between, or from information disclosed by, the parties at any time before or at the conclusion of the contract.
>
> (3) Neither the nationality of the parties nor the civil or commercial character of the parties or of the contract is to be taken into consideration in determining the application of this Convention.

---

45 The preamble of the CISG states, *inter alia* "BEING OF THE OPINION that the adoption of uniform rules which govern contracts for the international sale of goods and take into account the different social, economic and legal systems would contribute to the removal of legal barriers in international trade and promote the development of international trade". The CISG extracts models of civil law and common-law elements capable of harmonizing trade between countries of different legal traditions. *See* C. Samson, *supra* note 35; B. Goldman, *supra* note 35, pp. 177-192; E. Gaillard, *supra* note 35; B. Oppetit, *supra* note 35; B. Oppetit, *supra* note 35; P. Schlechriem & C. Witz, *supra* note 35; I. Schwenzer (Ed.), *supra* note 35.

46 C. Fountoulakis, *supra* note 17, p. 314; L. G. Meira Moser, *supra* note 18, p. 28.

The application of the CISG may occur independently (b) or by rules of private international law (c), as discussed below.

(b) The Direct Application of the CISG (Art. 1(1)(a))

As a general rule, the CISG applies to contracts for the sale of goods between parties whose places of business are in different states that have ratified the CISG, also called 'contracting' states.[47] Determining whether the CISG directly (and automatically) applies in such cases is straightforward. If either party has more than one place of business, then the place most closely related to the transaction is controlling and, in the absence of a place of business, the habitual residence.[48] If those places are both CISG contracting states, the contract is for the sale of goods and the parties have not opted out of its application, then the CISG applies to the parties' agreement.

Under these circumstances, a judge hearing a dispute between the parties should simply acknowledge that both are located in states that have ratified the CISG[49] and should apply the CISG as the law of their contract. The judge should do this even if the parties have specified one of their country's laws as the governing law of their agreement, unless in their agreement they have 'opted out' of the CISG by specifying that their choice of law excludes the application of the CISG.[50]

At first glance, this may seem to be in conflict with the parties' choice of law or superseding what the parties themselves agreed. In reality, however, it is an implementation of their choice because the CISG is incorporated into the domestic laws of both countries with respect to the international sale of goods.

---

47 CISG, Art 1. A list of contracting states can be found at https://uncitral.un.org/en/texts/salegoods/conventions/sale_of_goods/cisg/status.

48 *See* CISG, Art. 10:
    "For the purposes of this Convention:
    (a) if a party has more than one place of business, the place of business is that which has the closest relationship to the contract and its performance, having regard to the circumstances known to or contemplated by the parties at any time before or at the conclusion of the contract;
    (b) if a party does not have a place of business, reference is to be made to his habitual residence."

49 It is important to pay attention to the act of ratification, not the act of signature. Ratification involves the completion of internal legal and administrative procedures of each state for the instrument to be incorporated into domestic law, thereby generating legal effects. For this reason, the CISG provides in Art. 100 that the instrument applies to contracts concluded from the date of entry into force of the CISG. *See, e.g.* L.G. Meira Moser, *supra* note 13.

50 An example of an opt-out clause would be as follows: "This Contract is governed by the laws of […] without regard to the 1980 United Nations Convention on Contracts for the International Sale of Goods, the application of which is expressly excluded."

Take as an example the following case: the seller is in Texas, and the buyer is in Rome. The parties' contract contains a 'governing law' paragraph that states that the contract is governed by "the laws of the state of Texas, and any disputes shall be resolved in the courts of Harris County, Texas". The buyer defaults on payment. When the seller sues the buyer in the specified Texas court, the buyer asserts a defence under Texas laws regarding the sale of goods. Texas domestic law on the sale of goods differs from the CISG in some key respects. Is the CISG even relevant to this dispute?
a. No, because the parties expressly agreed that Texas law would apply to their contract.
b. Yes, because the United States has ratified the CISG, and the parties did not expressly exclude it from their contract, it is applicable law to the parties' contract.

The answer to the example above is that the CISG does indeed apply to the parties' contract and will be relevant to their dispute. If *both* companies to an international transaction involving the sale of goods are located in different contracting states (countries that have ratified the CISG), then the CISG applies *automatically*, unless the parties have expressly excluded it from their contract.

As its very name implies, the CISG applies to the sale of goods. It does *not* apply to contracts to provide services, although it will apply to contracts for delivery of both products and services unless the 'services' component (labour, engineering, etc.) makes up the preponderant part of the seller's obligations.[51]

In addition, by its own provisions the CISG does not apply to the sale of electricity. Nor does it apply to contracts that are ancillary to an international sales contract such as distribution agreements, contracts of carriage and insurance, or letters of credit. The CISG also does not apply to sales of ships, vessels or aircraft, or goods bought for personal, family or household use.[52] So, for example, a traveller from

---

51 *See* CISG, Art. 3:
   (1) Contracts for the supply of goods to be manufactured or produced are to be considered sales unless the party who orders the goods undertakes to supply a substantial part of the materials necessary for such manufacture or production.
   (2) This Convention does not apply to contracts in which the preponderant part of the obligations of the party who furnishes the goods consists in the supply of labour or other services.
52 *See* CISG, Art. 2:
   This Convention does not apply to sales:
   (a) of goods bought for personal, family or household use, unless the seller, at any time before or at the conclusion of the contract, neither knew nor ought to have known that the goods were bought for any such use;
   (b) by auction;
   (c) on execution or otherwise by authority of law;
   (d) of stocks, shares, investment securities, negotiable instruments or money;

France who purchased $20,000 of various consumer goods at the duty-free shop in Singapore International Airport could not assert a claim that his purchase was actually governed by the CISG and not Singapore law.

Silence in a contract on the issue of whether the governing law is subject to the CISG will generally lead to its application if the contract involves sales of products between parties located in different contracting states. Where the CISG might not otherwise apply, or where its application may be complex or uncertain (under Art. 1(1)(b), discussed below), the parties may choose to include it by the terms of their agreement.

The following would be sufficient to include the CISG, if that is what the parties wish:

> This Contract shall be governed by and construed under the 1980 United Nations Convention on Contracts for the International Sale of Goods, or, to the extent that the Convention does not settle the rights and obligations of the parties, the law of the State of Delaware.

To *exclude* the CISG from contracts where it would otherwise apply, however, parties must be explicit, as in the following: "This Contract shall be governed by the laws of the State of New York, not including the 1980 United Nations Convention on Contracts for the International Sale of Goods."

Of course, before accepting to have the CISG govern their contract or intentionally excluding its application, parties should consider whether the CISG offers particular advantages (or disadvantages) for potential disputes that may arise.[53]

(c) The Application of the CISG via Rules of Private International Law

The indirect application of the CISG – or by rules of private international law – involves complexities that are not as straightforward as the situation discussed above, where both parties to a transaction are from contracting states and the CISG applies automatically (unless expressly excluded).

Under Article 1(1)(b) of the CISG, 'private international law' may lead to its application if only *one* of the parties is from a contracting state, but the law of the contract or international choice of law rules also point to the law of a contracting state. This rule, however, should not apply where the contracting state made an 'Article 95 reservation' when it adopted the CISG, which permits countries to opt out of CISG Article 1(1)(b). For example, the United States is one of the CISG countries that made an Article 95 reservation when it ratified the CISG; France and Italy did not. For examples of how this can play out in international transactions, see Table 1.

 (e) of ships, vessels, hovercraft or aircraft;
 (f) of electricity.

53 For a discussion regarding the (dis)advantages of the CISG, *see* G. Moser, *supra* note 1, pp. 171-214.

Table 1 — Application of CISG by operation of 'private international law' (Art. 1(1)(b) of the Convention, except where contracting state has opted out by making Art. 95 reservation at time of treaty ratification)

Country of Party A	Country of Party B	Law of Contract	Would the CISG Apply?
United States – a CISG contracting state with Art. 95 reservation	United Kingdom – not a CISG contracting state	Law of France, a CISG contracting state	No
Italy – a CISG contracting state with no Art. 95 reservation	United Kingdom – not a CISG contracting state	Law of France, a CISG contracting state	Yes, because French domestic law includes the CISG

According to Article 1 paragraph (b), the CISG is the applicable law of international sales contract when a judge or arbitrator, while searching for the applicable law, concludes that it is the law of a contracting state. It seems therefore clear and intuitive that, in such a case, the law of the contract will be the CISG since, upon ratification, this legal framework joined the legal system of the state.

There is, however, a certain degree of complexity when the applicable law is that of a state that allows 'renvoi' to another state (a CISG contracting state). In addition to these complexities, it is necessary to verify whether the state made reservations upon ratification of the CISG. As we discussed earlier, at the time of ratification, the ratifying state enjoys certain powers and prerogatives, including that of not being bound by subparagraph (b) of Article 1(1), as provided for in Article 95 of CISG.[54] Under these circumstances, the CISG will not apply because the state that ratified has conditioned its ratification to non-binding effect of Article 1(1)(b). In this case, the CISG does not apply, but instead the law of the country determined by the conflict of laws rules that the judge or arbitrator will follow.

In such cases, if the judge or arbitrator, after using the conflict of laws rules available, concludes that the applicable law is the law of a contracting state, the CISG will not govern the contract between the parties.

If this appears complicated, keep in mind that the issues presented will arise mainly in situations in which the parties have not specified a governing law of their agreement.

---

54 *See* CISG, Art. 95:
   Any State may declare at the time of the deposit of its instrument of ratification, acceptance, approval or accession that it will not be bound by subparagraph (1)(b) of article 1 of this Convention.

Exercises: The Application (or Not) of the CISG

Exercise 2.6: Basic
Negotiations of contract between a seller in the Orinoco Belt (Venezuela) and a buyer in Hanoi (Vietnam) for the sale of kerosene are well under way and a first draft of the sales agreement is likely to be finalized in the next couple of days. The parties have agreed that the courts of Hanoi shall decide any disputes, but they have been unable to agree on the governing law that will apply to their contract and will leave this open as a result.

You are the international counsel advising the seller in this transaction. What are the main legal considerations you should examine before agreeing to this contract? What if you were advising the buyer in Hanoi?

Exercise 2.7: Basic
Assuming that in the same contract negotiation between the Venezuelan seller and the Viet buyer, both parties wish the CISG to apply to their contract, which of these governing law provisions could pose a problem for them and why?
a. A clause that simply elects Venezuelan or Vietnamese law as the governing law of the contract and is silent on the application of the CISG.
b. A clause that expressly specifies that the CISG shall apply.
c. A clause that specifies Venezuelan or Vietnamese law, specifically that either the Venezuelan or the Vietnamese domestic law for the sale of goods shall apply.

Exercise 2.8: Intermediate
Assume that after lengthy negotiations, the parties signed their contract in 2019. The choice of law provision reads as follows: "19. This contract shall be governed by the laws of the Bolivarian Republic of Venezuela". Venezuela signed the CISG in 1981. Vietnam ratified the CISG without reservations in 2015. Which law applies?
a. Domestic laws of Venezuela
b. Domestic laws of Vietnam
c. CISG
d. CISG, as supplemented by the Venezuelan law to the extent not addressed by the provisions of the CISG

Exercise 2.9: Intermediate
In addition to the choice of Venezuelan law as the governing law, in the spirit of compromise, the parties added this further provision on the choice of jurisdiction: "20. Any contractual disputes arising out of this contract shall be decided before the courts of Hanoi, Vietnam". Which law applies?
a) Domestic laws of Venezuela
b) Domestic laws on Vietnam
c) CISG

CHAPTER 2 NEGOTIATING CHOICE OF LAW CLAUSES

d) CISG, although the Hanoi court must now determine whether Vietnamese or Venezuelan law will supplement any matter not addressed by the provisions of the CISG

Exercise 2.10: Advanced

Assume the same factual elements of Exercise 2.2. Would your answer to Exercise 2.4 change if you were told that:
a. Venezuela had ratified the CISG in 2018?
b. Venezuela had ratified the CISG with reservation under Article 95?
c. Vietnam had ratified the CISG after the contract date?
d. Vietnam had ratified the CISG with reservations under Article 1(b)?
e. Vietnam had ratified the CISG with reservation under Articles 12 and 96 only?
f. Venezuela had not ratified the CISG; Vietnam and Venezuela had closely related legal rules on matters governed by the CISG; and Vietnam had ratified the CISG with reservation under Article 94(2) – for contracts of sale where parties have their places of business in Venezuela?
g. The contract was signed in 2014?
h. The contract was between a Vietnamese seller and a Venezuelan buyer?
i. The choice of jurisdiction clause reads as follows: "20. Any contractual disputes arising out of this contract shall be decided before the courts of the Bolivarian Republic of Venezuela".

Exercise 2.11: Intermediate

Assume the same facts as in Exercises 2.6 to 2.10, but in this case instead of providing for the courts at the buyer's principal place of business (Vietnam), the parties would like to agree that disputes will be decided by arbitration with Singapore as the seat. In this case, rank the following factors in the order you would consider most critical:
a. Conflict of laws rules typically applied by courts in Vietnam and Venezuela
b. Venezuelan environmental laws
c. *Ad hoc* vs. institutional arbitration
d. Ratification of the United Nations Convention on the Recognition and Enforcement of Foreign Arbitral Awards (The 1958 New York Convention) by Vietnam and Venezuela
e. National arbitration in Vietnam and Venezuela, before agreeing to either as a legal seat
f. The reputation of the courts of Singapore towards arbitration

Exercises: Advanced

This section provides exercises for you to design your own choice of law clause and the legal frameworks to govern your contract.

CHAPTER 2 NEGOTIATING CHOICE OF LAW CLAUSES

Exercise 2.12
Negotiation of a contract between a Swiss seller and a Hong Kong buyer for the sale of precious metal watches. The parties have been trading for a number of years and would like to prepare a comprehensive legal framework within which to bind future agreements between the parties. You were given the following summary of their prior dealings:

a. The parties have had a successful record of dealings so far. Contracts have been made in writing and minor amendments, when strictly necessary, have been performed orally.

b. As regards the mechanics of the contract negotiation, the buyer would enquire the seller as to the availability of the precious metal watches. The seller would then reply following which the buyer would place an order. In case of substantial amendments or cancellations of any orders by any of the parties, this has been made in writing (letter or email), generally within 7 days from the date of the order, although they had one case (treated as exceptional) where the order was cancelled by seller 10 days after the order had been placed by the buyer (due to shortage of the product in stock). Whenever the goods arrived later than expected or the goods were not suitable as agreed, seller informed it to the buyer in writing no later than 15 days from receipt of the goods. In the rare cases of goods arriving later than expected, buyer accepted the goods whenever there was no 'emergency' to receive the items. However, when the buyer made it unequivocal to the seller that it needed the goods within the time frame agreed, the late receipt resulted in the goods been returned to the seller, at the seller's own expenses.

c. In cases of replacements for deficient goods, they have agreed to reduce the total price to be paid by the buyer who recalls that there have been cases where the product did not satisfy the intended qualities and therefore, the buyer, once informed, promptly reimbursed the amount paid by the seller in some cases sharing the shipping fees and bank charges whenever the buyer's order was unclearly placed. This has been made by email and the deduction ranged from 10 to 25% of the total price, depending on these circumstances: (i) time spent by the buyer to inform the seller (typically no more than 15 days); (ii) price of the contract; (iii) type of goods and (iv) other unforeseen circumstances. As to the orders and payments, the buyer typically places orders by email (orally is an exception in this industry sector – in this case, both parties exchange emails to record it within a reasonable time) and pays within a period of 5 days after notification from the seller that the goods have been dispatched.

d. The seller has had instances where the buyer asked to pay upon delivery, although rarely, in which case the seller accepted such request, bearing in mind, in particular, the price of the contract (never over USD 100,000) and in order to maintain the good relationship with the buyer. As to the completion of the purchase, the buyer recalls that on three occasions they renegotiated the payment conditions and price due to market fluctuations. Finally, the buyer has had cases where the goods could not be shipped as previously agreed due to strikes and unfavourable weather conditions in the port of Genoa, Italy, from where the goods are shipped.

Outline the main choice of law considerations.

Exercise 2.13
Consider the factual background in Exercise 2.12. The parties wish to continue trading on the basis of the above practices and would like these practices to govern any future deal between them without recourse to any applicable laws. You are required to elaborate the skeleton of this legal framework.

Exercise 2.14
Following Exercise 2.13, set out as bullet points the important matters that should be considered for drafting and using this legal framework.

Exercise 2.15
Negotiation of contract between a biotechnology company based in California (United States) and a Pharma company based in Aachen (Germany) for the development and commercialization of a therapeutic protein. The US company has recently discovered a therapeutic protein from açaí palm trees and is looking to protect and commercialize this protein. The German company routinely cooperates in the development and marketing of therapeutic proteins around the world.
Before proposing a particular law to govern this contract, draft a checklist of legal risks and red flags you think could arise in the event of any dispute. What are the most likely breaches of contract that may be committed by the seller or the buyer?

Exercise 2.16
Following Exercise 2.15, the parties are now negotiating the choice of law that will govern their contract. They would like the domestic laws of California to apply without the application of any other laws or rules of law, save for Part II of the CISG which both parties consider to be advantageous and a good compromise. Assuming any disputes will be decided by arbitration, explain whether you think the arbitrators will have any difficulty implementing this choice of law.

Exercise 2.17
Following Exercise 2.16, draft this choice of law clause.

Notes

CHAPTER 2 NEGOTIATING CHOICE OF LAW CLAUSES

Chapter 3 Negotiating Methods of Dispute Resolution

> **Learning Objectives**
> - When there is no contractual choice of forum for resolving disputes
> - Courts vs. arbitration? Issues of enforceability, expertise of decision-makers in technical matters and confidentiality
> - The contractual arbitration clause
>   - Institutional vs. *ad hoc* arbitration
>   - The choice of the arbitral institution
>   - The elements of an arbitration clause
> - The exercises in this chapter are aimed at developing successful legal and negotiation strategies for contract choice of forum clauses.

We have already seen the complications that can arise when parties do not agree on the choice of law of a contract and inject even more uncertainty by not agreeing on a place and method for resolving any disputes. Failure to agree on dispute resolution, or failing to articulate it in a clear and binding way, can lead to its own wasteful and expensive litigation. When there is ambiguity over the place and method of resolving disputes, a claimant must file in a location and then, if the respondent does not agree with the selection, fight to remain in that forum. And even when the claimant wins this jurisdictional battle, it can leave doubts over the enforceability of the outcome.

This is a pity, because parties negotiating an international commercial contract will almost always have at their disposal many different procedures that they can agree to resolve any disputes. The questions, therefore, should be how parties should (a) choose the best method resolving conflicts to propose for inclusion in a cross-border contract, including the adequacy of any particular forum for resolving and enforcing the outcome,[55] and (b) assess the potential consequences of accepting a compromise solution in order to reach agreement with the other party?

---

55 'Forum' is used throughout to refer to arbitration or a national court.

CHAPTER 3 NEGOTIATING METHODS OF DISPUTE RESOLUTION

These are two of the most frequent issues to arise in cross-border contract negotiations. This chapter should help build skills in addressing them.

To reiterate, the absence of an agreement on where and how to resolve disputes will require the parties to ask a number of difficult questions should a dispute arise. For example, where should I bring a legal action? What are the risks and costs involved if a court declines jurisdiction? What will happen if the other party initiates proceedings simultaneously in a different forum? These issues of jurisdiction can involve the application of various country Civil Procedure Codes, Acts, and Regulations. If the place and method for resolving a dispute are not clearly identified in the parties' agreement, even sophisticated international commercial lawyers may have difficulty predicting where and how the dispute will ultimately be decided and whether the result will be enforceable.

Despite the critical need to get dispute resolution right in an international commercial contract, parties are frequently unaware of the consequences of failing to agree on a forum or of choosing a court without considering how they may need to enforce their contractual rights.[56]

3.1 The Default Rule: Suing the Defendant in the Courts of Their Home Location

Generally, a party may always be sued in the country where it has its registered office or where it undertakes its main business. Of course, there are exceptions to this, and many instances where courts may decline to hear a case where the alleged breach or contractual performance was rendered in another country. By the same reasoning, the courts of the other country may retain jurisdiction if, in their view, there is a sufficient connection with the transaction, even though the defending party is not located there.[57] Further, the absence of agreement means the enforceability of any judgment in another country will be a matter for investigation and, often, speculation, which may inject uncertainty, delays and costs.[58]

All of this creates uncertainty for the parties for the important issue of whether they can enforce their contractual rights. To avoid this uncertainty, parties will almost always want to include in their contract a clause that clearly states where and how any disputes arising under the contract will be resolved.

---

56 G. Moser, 'Brexit, Cognitive Biases and the Jurisdictional Conundrum', *Kluwer Arbitration Blog*, 15 December 2018, available at http://arbitrationblog.kluwerarbitration.com/2018/12/15/brexit-cognitive-biases-and-the-jurisdictional-conundrum/; and G. Moser, *supra* note 1, pp. 155-156.
57 *Id.*
58 G. Moser, *supra* note 1, pp. 134-140.

3.2 The Effect of the Hague Convention on the Choice of Courts

The Hague Convention on Choice of Court (hereinafter the *Hague Convention*), concluded in 2005, and which came into force on 1 October 2015,[59] was designed to give effect to the parties' choice of court agreements and resulting judgments.[60] The Hague Convention has three main pillars: Article 5, which provides that the chosen court must hear the dispute; Article 6, which prevents any court not chosen by the parties from proceeding with a hearing (the court must suspend or dismiss proceedings), thus the other contracting state must abstain from asserting jurisdiction over the claim; and Article 8, which provides that judgment given by the chosen court must be recognized and enforced by the courts of the other contracting states.[61]

In practical terms, if a party agrees to have a contractual dispute heard in a court of a signatory state, this choice (and any resulting judgment) will be given full effect in the courts of all other signatory states.[62] On the date of this publication, the Hague Convention counts 32 states bound to it.[63]

3.3 Why a Party May Prefer to Designate the Courts

There are a number of reasons for which parties may prefer to initiate proceedings in the courts of a given country.

Sometimes parties will insist on resolving disputes in their home country's courts simply because they have no choice. This is sometimes the case with state-owned or public enterprises that are subject to laws or inflexible company rules that require them to resolve any contract disputes in the local courts.

But most often, contracting parties will typically default to a more basic justification for selecting their home courts, which is that they will be 'playing at home' or simply not 'at the opponent's home'. Sometimes this preference for local

---

59 Further information is available at the website of the Hague Conference on Private International Law (www.hcch.net/en/home).

60 The full text of the Hague Convention is available at www.hcch.net/en/instruments/conventions/full-text/?cid=98.

61 There might be some friction if the member state made a declaration under Art. 19 of the Hague Convention, which allows a court of a contracting state to decline to hear the dispute if it has no connection with the dispute or the parties. In the author's view, this is a most unfortunate provision and one that contradicts the nature of cross-border contracts and cross-border litigation to that effect, i.e. the search for a neutral forum to hear disputes. That said, none of the member states has made such declaration. Nevertheless, Art. 32 of the Hague Convention authorizes member states to make (and modify) an Art. 19 declaration at any time.

62 G. Moser, *supra* note 1, pp. 155-158.

63 Further information is available at www.hcch.net/en/instruments/conventions/status-table/?cid=98.

courts will also be based on perceptions of a perceived superiority: of the rules of civil procedure and of evidence; of the fact that – in many countries – judicial proceedings are relatively inexpensive compared with arbitration; the party's familiarity with the courts in that legal system, a preference for the language to be used, the court's reputation as a quality decision-maker, the strength of the profession and institutions at the court's seat and the ease of enforcing a judgment in the same country as the courts.[64]

If they do not wish to consider arbitration (discussed below), parties may sometimes compromise by choosing the courts of a third jurisdiction. While sometimes this will offer an effective middle ground, it can often add unnecessary uncertainty on whether the court will accept jurisdiction or how it will apply the law, especially if that law is different from the one where the court is located.[65] For example, a court may decide it lacks jurisdiction over the parties or their dispute with which it has no connection. As noted in Chapter 2, judges may be reluctant to apply a foreign law with which they are unfamiliar and may default to national laws that regulate contracts that may take both parties by surprise.[66] Parties can at least reach agreement by compromise, but in doing so they should try to reduce the potential for unintended consequences.

3.4   Considerations When Proposing or Accepting Courts as the Forum

Before specifying the courts of a given country as the forum to resolve disputes, parties to an international commercial contract should first ask whether they have any contract objectives or likely disputes that may be affected. For example, what are the core goals of the contract of concerns for which the party is likely to want certainty? Payment, limitations of liability, warranty, suspension or termination rights? Is it likely the party will want or need to enforce the judgment in another country? Would a potential interim relief or injunction be beneficial and enforceable in other countries? Given these and any other conditions, would arbitration be a better choice?

---

64   L. Silberman & F. Ferrari, 'Getting to the Law Applicable to the Merits in International Arbitration and the Consequences of Getting it Wrong', *NYU Law and Economics Research Paper No. 10-40*, 2010, pp. 1-34.

65   As L. Spagnolo exemplifies, if a choice of forum clause fails to attain the intended result, it may affect the efficacy of the choice of law. The chosen law may unexpectedly become a foreign law to be proven as fact and applied by a tribunal unfamiliar with that law – both a costly and risky exercise. *See* L. Spagnolo, 'Green Eggs and Ham: The CISG, Path Dependence, and the Behavioural Economics of Lawyers' Choices of Law in International Sales Contracts', *Journal of Private International Law*, Vol. 6, 2009, pp. 417-464, p. 437; L. Spagnolo, *CISG Exclusion and Legal Efficiency*, Wolters Kluwer, Alphen aan den Rijn, 2014, pp. 191-192.

66   G. Moser, *supra* note 1, p. 132.

In deciding the dispute resolution method best suited to the contract objectives, parties should also consider forum convenience and 'contract enforcement costs', i.e. the costs of enforcing what has been contractually agreed. Courts, especially, will not have flexibility to conduct hearings at the convenience of parties and their counsel and enforcing their judgments in other countries may add substantial additional time and costs.[67]

Exercise: Intermediate

Exercise 3.1: Damages from Multiple Tort Claims; Where to Sue the Defendant for Breach of Contract?

The seller is a supplier of personnel who performs various marine-related services and is headquartered in Mexico City. The seller's lead sales manager flew to Miami to negotiate and sign a large contract to supply personnel and support services to the buyer, a Miami company that operates a fleet of cruise ships. The contract provides that all personnel supplied will be "suitably trained for their roles and all key personnel, which expressly include all positions of captain and first officers, shall have a minimum of 15 years experience in navigational roles on cruise ships or equivalent marine operations". There is no choice of law or choice of forum clause in the contract.

Unfortunately, one of the buyer's cruise ships partially sunk off the coast of Brazil after the captain sailed too close to shore, causing injury to many passengers. The company has reached settlements with all but 32 passengers, who have instead asserted claims in different national courts. Seventeen have sued the cruise ship company in the courts of São Paulo as the closest court to the accident; 10 have sued in the courts of Miami where the cruise ship company is headquartered; and 5 have sued in the courts of New York, the place where they bought the tickets.

For damages to its ship and any liability to the passengers, the Miami cruise ship company believes it has a strong claim against the Mexican company that supplied the captain and other personnel.

You are counsel to the Miami cruise ship company. Please list the possible advantages or disadvantages of asserting claims against the Mexican company in each of the following jurisdictions, especially with respect to whether the courts will accept jurisdiction, the ability to prove your client's case and damages, and any concerns about enforcing a favourable outcome. Assume there is no enforcement treaty in existence between any of the countries involved. Which court would you recommend to your client?

a. Mexico City, as the seller's place of residence;
b. São Paulo, as the place in the country of the accident, the place where the contract was being performed at the time the claim arose and where most of the personal injury claims are pending;

---

67 *Id.*, p. 153.

c. Miami, as the buyer's place of residence and the place where the contract was negotiated; or
d. São Paulo, Miami and New York, asserting claims against the Mexican seller as a third-party defendant in the existing litigations brought by the passengers.

Variation 1: Assume that the Mexican defendant has assets only in Mexico. How might this affect your advice to your client on the best place to sue?

Variation 2: Assume that the contract for the supply of marine personnel provided for the parties to resolve any disputes by arbitration in London. Where would you suggest your client file a claim against the Mexican company for damages arising from the injured passengers and why?

Exercise: Basic

Exercise 3.2: Breach of Contract and Specification of Courts

A contract between a Latvian seller and a German buyer for the sale of glass fibre contains a dispute resolution clause which reads as follows: "8. Any disputes arising out of this contract shall be decided before the courts of Latvia." The Latvian seller claims that the German buyer breached the contract by failing to pay the amounts due. Where should the Latvian seller file its claim?
a. Latvia, according to the contract clause on disputes.
b. Germany, where the buyr resides and has all of its assets.

Exercise: Intermediate

Exercise 3.3: Enforcement Strategy for Court Decisions

Negotiation of contract between a Brazilian seller and a Portuguese buyer for the sale of raw sugar. The contract contains a dispute resolution clause which reads as follows: "10.2. Any disputes arising out of this contract shall be decided before the courts of Portugal." The buyer wishes to terminate the contract and seek damages. The seller has assets in Angola and Mozambique.

As counsel for the buyer, how could the existence of an Agreement of Legal and Judicial Cooperation between Portugal and either Angola or Mozambique assist you to develop a strategy to enforce a potential favourable court decision in Portugal? Please provide a short explanation that you would present to your client.

If you could change the contract to have a different place and method for resolving disputes, what would you recommend?

Exercise 3.4: Some Costs and Complications of Litigating in a Foreign Court – Basic

The seller is an internet company in Toronto, Canada, that is negotiating to sell search engine optimization (SEO) services for $10 million to an internet-based seller of consumer goods headquartered in China, but with principal markets in the United Kingdom, Australia and North America. The current draft of the contract

the parties are negotiating states that any disputes shall be resolved in the courts of the PRC (People's Republic of China). One risk of litigation is that the Chinese buyer could file a claim in court in Beijing demanding the return of the entire $10 million paid to the Canadian company or even damages on the grounds that the technical specifications were not met. Assuming that the parties are confident in that the Chinese court will be impartial regarding the presence of a Chinese party, explain how the following might pose problems during the course of the proceedings and for which party, the Chinese buyer or the Canadian seller or both?
a. Translations
b. Enforcement
c. The judge's technical expertise
d. Travel costs

Variation: Draft a short, one-paragraph email to the counsel for the Chinese company providing reasons both parties should prefer dispute resolution in a different court or arbitration in English.

Exercise 3.5: Goods in Transit – Basic
A contract between a buyer in London (United Kingdom) and a seller in N'Djamena (Chad) provides for the sale of resins *ex works* (delivered at the place of manufacture) in Chad, after which the seller will ship them to the United Kingdom from the port of Tunis (Tunisia). The contract states it is governed by the laws of England and Wales but does not have a choice of forum clause or any provision regarding resolution of disputes. The seller has delivered the goods to the port in Tunis but a strike has arisen and they cannot be shipped to the United Kingdom. Where should the buyer file a legal action if it wants to take possession of the goods?
a. The judicial courts in N'Djamena
b. The judicial courts in Tunis
c. The judicial courts in London

Variation 1: If instead the goods were shipped to the United Kingdom but retained in customs in the port of Dover (United Kingdom), where would the buyer file a legal action to take possession?

Variation 2: After receiving the resins, the buyer notices that there are a number of non-conformities, which the seller refuses to compensate. Where should the buyer file a legal action to collect damages from the seller?

Exercise 3.6: Goods in Transit – Intermediate
Your client is a seller in Dubai (United Arab Emirates) and you are representing them in contract negotiations with a buyer in Singapore. The contract is for the sale of gold to be shipped from the port of Sohar (Oman) and paid in two instalments: 10% at the time of shipping and 90% at the time of the buyer's receipt of the goods. The parties failed to agree on a choice of forum clause for the contract, so there is no

agreed place of dispute resolution. If the buyer defaults on the second payment, where should the seller file a legal action to receive the sums it is owed?
a. The judicial courts in Dubai
b. The judicial courts in Singapore
c. The judicial courts in Sohar

Variation: Shortly after paying the first instalment, the price of gold plummeted in the international markets. To avoid making the second payment, the buyer filed a court action in the courts of Singapore seeking a court order to prevent the seller from delivering the goods. Assuming the seller wishes the buyer to take delivery, in which court should the seller take action or respond? Can you advise the seller on a court strategy to protect its financial interests against the defaulting buyer?

Exercise 3.7: Intermediate
Consider the above factual background in the contract for the sale of gold. You were retained by the buyer to file a court action against the seller, but the information shared with you is that the goods are indeed in Sohar. Describe why each of following factors may be relevant (or not) to a court action strategy and why.
1) Applicable law
2) Place in which the breach occurred
3) Place of performance
4) Place mostly connected with the contract
5) Place of parties' registered office

Exercise 3.8: Basic
A Mexican buyer and a Brazilian seller entered into a sales contract. The parties have elected the courts of Mexico to hear any contractual dispute. The seller claims the buyer breached the contract by failing to open a letter of credit before delivery. Where should the seller file its legal action for damages from breach of contract?
a. Brazil
b. Mexico

Exercise 3.9: Advanced
The contract is between a Brazilian seller and a Portuguese buyer for the sale of raw sugar. The contract contains a dispute resolution clause, which reads as follows: "10.2. Any contractual disputes arising out of this contract shall be decided before the courts of Portugal." The buyer wishes to terminate the contract and claim damages. An asset-tracing company has found that the seller, although a Brazilian legal entity, has assets only in Angola and Mozambique. As counsel for the buyer, explain to your client the steps you would recommend in order to enforce a favourable court judgment, assuming you will be able to obtain one.
a. Describe the steps that can be taken without retaining local counsel in any of the countries.

b. Describe additional steps with advice from local country counsel, and the countries for which you would recommend seeking this advice.

3.4.1 Alternatives to the Courts: Mediation and Arbitration Clauses

Although agreements on how to resolve disputes may be (and often are) part of the parties' main contract, they are independent from the terms of the main contract and survive its termination or breach due to the separability presumption. In other words, even if the main contract is declared null and void, or unenforceable, the agreement on how to resolve disputes remains effective.[68] As a result, even after the contractual relations between the parties have ended, their agreement on how to resolve disputes will continue. In international commercial contracts, these are generally divided into two categories of procedures: those that result in a binding outcome even if the parties disagree and those that will only lead to a binding result if the parties agree.

The first category, procedures that will bind the parties even if they do not agree on the outcome, consists of litigation in the public (state) courts or arbitration. The second category, procedures that lead to a binding outcome only upon agreement, are various forms of negotiation and mediation.[69] Importantly, an agreement to mediate will only complement an arbitration clause or agreement to submit disputes to a court for resolution; it will not replace the need for a form of binding dispute resolution.

If an international contract does not specify *any* method of binding resolution, the contract itself should still be valid, at least in theory. But, as discussed earlier,[70] the uncertainty over which courts will have jurisdiction over disputes may leave one or both sides unhappy about whether or how the contract will be enforced in the event of any disputes.

> *Exercise 3.10: Basic*
>
> João and Astrid are negotiating a contract for the sale of aircraft engine parts from São Paulo, Brazil, where João's company manufactures them, and Elblag, a small town in northern Poland, where the airline Astrid works for is headquartered. The contract will provide for full payment to be remitted within 90 days of the parts

---

[68] The separability presumption is recognized under most national arbitration laws and arbitration rules worldwide. *See, e.g.* 1985 UNCITRAL Model Law on International Commercial Arbitration, Art. 16.

[69] In some countries, mediation exists separately from a procedure known as *conciliation*, in which a neutral third party proposes an outcome that the parties can agree to accept. For the purposes of this book, we refer only to mediation, as the term is typically used in international commercial dispute resolution, i.e., a facilitative process by which a neutral third party assists the parties towards reaching a settlement of their dispute.

[70] *See* pp. 40-44 *supra*.

being declared available for delivery *ex works* (as defined by INCOTERMS) at the seller's factory in Brazil.[71]

Astrid is insisting that the contract should only have a requirement to negotiate disputes and no binding procedure. She explains that her company prefers to maintain a collaborative partnership with their suppliers and that they always have been able to resolve disputes through negotiations. Going to arbitration or the courts in a dispute with a key supplier would be considered a failure of the commercial relationship. Her proposed dispute resolution clause is the following: "In the event of any dispute under this contract, the parties will negotiate in good faith to reach an amicable resolution."

João must report to his company on whether to accept the contract without specifying any form of binding dispute resolution procedure.

a. What do you think should be the biggest concern to João's company in accepting the contract as Astrid is proposing?
b. In no more than a single paragraph, identify problems that might arise in the event the parties are unable to resolve a dispute by negotiation.
c. If Astrid will not change her position, are there ways that could mitigate the main risk to João's company?

3.5 The Benefits of Neutrality, Efficiency and Enforceability of Mediation and Arbitration in International Commercial Contracts

Parties often choose mediation and arbitration in their international commercial contracts to avoid local court procedures and to bring neutrality into the proceedings, especially where one (or sometimes both) of the contracting parties distrusts the available court options. But arbitration – and increasingly mediation – offers an additional crucial feature for contracts, which is their enforceability across borders.

For arbitration, cross-border enforceability is largely the result of the 1958 United Nations Convention on the Recognition and Enforcement of Foreign Arbitral Awards ("the New York Convention"[72]). The effect of the New York Convention is, in theory, to give arbitration award the legal effect of a judgment of the court of first instance in the country of enforcement, which is any of the 166 states that have ratified it. In practice, a creditor's ability to enforce an international arbitration award will always depend on the quality, neutrality and efficiency of the convention states where enforcement is sought. Still, this feature of the New York Convention – enforceability – has since 1958 rendered arbitral awards as more valuable internationally than domestic court judgments.

---

71 This means that legal title to the goods will pass to the buyer once the seller declares them available for pick up at its factory. *See* https://iccwbo.org/resources-for-business/incoterms-rules/incoterms-rules-2010/.

72 The text of the 1958 New York Convention is available at www.uncitral.org/pdf/english/texts/arbitration/NY-conv/New-York-Convention-E.pdf.

Mediation, too, is a means of reducing the risk and uncertainty of resolving disputes in courts and can also reduce substantially the cost of international commercial disputes. As a dispute resolution procedure, it often appears to be more similar to negotiation than to litigation or arbitration. As a result, it is generally easy for parties to seek to resolve a dispute through mediation even though they may have no familiarity with international arbitration (or the courts of other countries). Not surprisingly, it is common today for parties to an international commercial contract to include a requirement to attempt to resolve their dispute through mediation before submitting it to arbitration or court litigation. Further, all of the major international arbitration institutions today also offer mediation services (and often standard mediation-arbitration dispute resolution clauses), so that parties do not need to specify different institutions rules if they want to include both in their contracts.

Until 2019, however, international mediation lacked the additional advantage of the cross-border enforceability available to arbitral awards. This is now changing, with the introduction of the United Nations Convention on the Enforcement of Mediated Settlement Agreements (the 'Singapore Convention'). The Singapore Convention came into effect on 12 September 2020, after having been ratified by five countries and with the others having indicated their intention to join the convention soon.[73]

Another legal development of note concerning the cooperation of foreign court judgments is the Convention on the Recognition and Enforcement of Foreign Judgments in Civil or Commercial Matters of 2 July 2019 (the 'Judgments Convention'), concluded by the Hague Conference of Private International law. The Judgments Convention provides for the mutual enforcement of court judgments, not limited to exclusive jurisdiction clauses, and sets out uniform rules to facilitate the effective recognition and enforcement of such judgments.[74] The Judgments Convention has no contracting parties to date.

3.5.1 Other Reasons Parties Specify Mediation in Their International Contracts

An often-overlooked value of including a requirement of mediation in an international contract is that it can mitigate a party's concerns over the risks posed by the contract's binding form of dispute resolution. In the best of cases, the parties will reduce to zero the risk of imperfect dispute resolution by settling instead of initiating formal proceedings that may appear less than ideal.

Even when they do not settle, the parties will have a better understanding of their dispute by virtue of having met and attempted to resolve their differences in

---

[73] The full text of the Singapore Convention is available at https://uncitral.un.org/en/texts/mediation/conventions/international_settlement_agreements. *See also* www.singaporeconvention.org/.

[74] The full text of the Judgments Convention is available at www.hcch.net/en/projects/legislative-projects/judgments.

mediation. And the attempt to resolve their differences amicably, before initiating formal proceedings, may help preserve important relationships where they exist with opposing parties.

The confidentiality of mediation is another attraction of the procedure, presenting parties with the opportunity to openly address the causes of their contractual dispute, without concern that their candour will be used against them in subsequent proceedings if a settlement is not reached. Further, whereas judges and arbitrators are limited to the cause of action and, therefore, would mainly award damages to compensate for the other party's breach, parties in a mediation may be able to use the process to identify ways to alter their contractual relationship to provide for mutually satisfactory solutions, such as agreeing to sell or purchase additional products or services or adopt discounts or advance payments.

3.5.2 Other Reasons Parties Specify Arbitration in Their International Contracts

While most parties will consider neutrality, efficiency and enforceability as their primary reasons for including an arbitration clause in their international contracts, they may also be driven by certain procedural advantages that it offers. One frequently mentioned advantage is the confidentiality of the arbitration process.

While it is true that arbitration is not a 'public' procedure, in the sense of court room dramas as portrayed in Hollywood films, it is not entirely true that it is 'confidential' as most people use the term. Arbitration *proceedings* are not typically public in international commercial cases, in the sense that only the parties and their counsel have access to the written pleadings and oral hearings. But there is rarely any sanction for sharing this information with others. Further, any parallel court proceedings during the arbitration or any subsequent attempt to enforce the ensuing award will be achieved through the courts, potentially making both aspects of the proceedings and award itself part of the public record.

Thus, if a party wishes to treat certain information in their commercial contract as 'confidential', or the entirety of the contract itself, they should make this a substantive obligation in their contract, with sanctions for breach. The parties may also wish to choose a set of institutional rules that provide appropriate protection required, which could include specific costs (or otherwise) sanctions for such breaches.

3.5.3 The Elements of an Arbitration Clause

An agreement to arbitrate in a contract, usually called an arbitration clause, will typically contain four main components: (a) the submission or reference of disputes to arbitration (the most important of the four); (b) the important ingredients of the place (or seat), rules and language of the arbitration; (c) optional features that are not necessary but which the parties may choose to include to customize the arbitration to their particular desires and (d) any requirement to consider or attempt mediation.

3.5.4 The Agreement to Submit Disputes to Arbitration

To be valid, an arbitration clause must ensure that any disputes will be resolved by arbitration rather than by a national court. Typical wording is 'all disputes arising out of or in connection with this contract'. This language covers claims based on the contract or with a contractual connection, such as a tort claim or one based on other extra-contractual theories. This language covers claims or defences that the contract is not valid or was terminated.

In all events, the referral to arbitration should use clear, direct language that leaves no hint that the parties intended arbitration to be simply an option. For example, if the parties say that any disputes 'may be referred' to arbitration, they may present a recalcitrant party with the argument that they may also submit disputes to the courts. It would be much better to say that disputes 'shall be referred to arbitration', which is not ambiguous.

Sometimes, parties use redundant verbiage that is still very broad and general, such as "all disputes, disagreements, claims, or controversies". This probably does not introduce any ambiguity or undermine the agreement to arbitrate, but it does not really add anything of value, either.

Sometimes, however, parties can unintentionally harm the validity of the arbitration clause by using more specific language that reduces the scope of disputes the arbitrators can decide. For example, the parties might adopt language such as "all disputes concerning the interpretation or performance of this contract" thinking this will include all disputes arising out of the contract. But does this language also cover a claim or defence concerning the termination of the contract or whether the contract ever came into force? If the parties still want the additional language of a 'belts and suspenders' approach, they would be wise to also combine it with the general language instead of replacing it. A clause that includes both general and specific language might read, for example, "all disputes arising out of or in connection with this contract *including, without limitation, disputes concerning the interpretation or performance of this contract*".[75]

> **Exercise 3.11: Basic**
>
> João persuaded Astrid to include an arbitration clause in their contract. Although they are still negotiating the seat of arbitration and the applicable rules and other details of the clause, they have agreed to adopt the standard phrasing, "all disputes arising out of or in connection with this contract shall be resolved by arbitration". João's boss, however, has expressed concerns that this language is not broad enough to cover a situation in which Astrid's company claims the contract was never valid to begin with. He told João to change the language to "all disputes relating to the formation of this contract or its performance shall be settled by arbitration": Astrid has rejected this proposed language.
>
> What should João tell his boss?

---

75   *See* M. Mcilwrath & J. Savage, *supra* note 8, pp. 1.013-16; 1.019.

CHAPTER 3 NEGOTIATING METHODS OF DISPUTE RESOLUTION

  a. Astrid's position is unreasonable and João's company should reject the contract because her company cannot be trusted. They want to be able to terminate the contract on the grounds that it never came into force and avoid any liability for breaching any of its terms.
  b. The original language already addresses the sort of dispute his boss is concerned about, over whether the contract was validly entered into, and its broader scope is probably even better for João's company if there is a concern about Astrid's company terminating or breaching the contract.

Exercise 3.12: Basic
Astrid has now come back with a proposal to include the language that João's boss has requested, but only as an addition to the originally proposed wording. The new language would read, "all disputes arising out of or in connection with this contract, including any disputes relating to its validity or formation, shall be settled by arbitration": Should João find this acceptable and why?
  a. Yes
  b. No

3.6   Emergency or Interim Measures of Protection

Sometimes parties will want their agreement to arbitrate to also permit them to seek urgent, interim relief in court. Specifying the court's jurisdiction to hear emergency measures is not always necessary, since courts will typically retain this power, but the parties may feel safer if they clearly state this.

Exercise 3.13: Intermediate
Before executing the contract with Astrid's company, João decided he should ask his company's intellectual property counsel to review it. His colleague provided several comments, including on the scope of the arbitration. She explained that many of the aircraft parts that the company will be selling into Poland involve valuable intellectual property in the form of trade secrets that are not covered by patents. What if Astrid's company shares that technology with a competitor? She is concerned that an arbitration will only provide for damages and will not prevent the loss of technology leadership and market share. What can João suggest to address her concerns?
  a. Abandon the arbitration agreement and insist instead on disputes being decided in the courts, although exactly *which* court is hard to say.
  b. Keep arbitration as the form for resolving disputes but include a statement that the agreement to arbitrate is "without prejudice to either party's right to seek at any time emergency or conservatory measures of protection in any court having jurisdiction".
  c. Add an additional clause for resolving technical and intellectual property disputes, which will be decided by an expert and which will be conducted separately from the arbitration.

3.7   The Seat or Place of Arbitration

There are very few elements that must be included in an international arbitration clause, and the place (or 'seat') of arbitration is one, and almost always the most important. It is the city to which the arbitration is legally attached, which has three major legal consequences by providing the procedural law to govern the arbitration, the courts that will support the arbitration or hear an action to set aside the award and the 'nationality' of the award, which is important for enforcement purposes.

The specified place of arbitration, however, is not the same as the location where an institution whose rules will be used is headquartered or even where hearings will be conducted. Regardless of the city they have chosen as the place of arbitration in their agreement, the parties are free to choose the arbitration rules of any institution and even conduct hearings in any city they (or the arbitrators) prefer. For example, Article 14(2) of the ICC Rules expressly permits arbitral tribunals to hold 'hearings and meetings' wherever it considers appropriate, after consultation with the parties (and provided the parties have or agreed otherwise). Similarly, Article 16.3 of the London Court of International Arbitration (LCIA) Rules 2014 and 2020 allows arbitral tribunals to hold hearings 'at any convenient geographical place in consultation with the parties'. There are often good reasons to hold hearings in a different city or country than the one specified in the parties' agreement as the 'place of arbitration', including issues regarding accessibility (such as visa requirements), personal safety (where the location may be problematic) or simply because a different location is more convenient and less expensive for all participants. As a practical matter, however, the venue for most arbitration hearings is typically the same as the 'place of arbitration' designated in the parties' arbitration agreement, even if there is no formal requirement for this to be so.

> *Exercise 3.14: Basic*
> Chiara is negotiating with an English company and she would prefer to include a clause providing for arbitration outside the United Kingdom, but the English company is insisting on arbitration under the rules of the LCIA, with London as the place of arbitration. Is it possible for Chiara's company to agree to LCIA arbitration, but with the place of arbitration (the seat) in another country? If Chiara accepts London as the place of arbitration, can the arbitration hearings be held elsewhere, such as in Milan, where Chiara and her client are based?

> *Exercise 3.15: Intermediate*
> The parties' agreement specified that any disputes would be resolved by arbitration under the ICC rules and that the place of arbitration would be Jeddah, Saudi Arabia. After a dispute arose, the parties nominated a tribunal consisting of three arbitrators: one of whom is a well-known English arbitrator, who happens to be a woman; another is man who is a Qatari citizen and the third is a Canadian but who has an Israeli stamp in his passport. All three have difficulties obtaining visas for

travel into Saudi Arabia for a hearing. What is the most likely solution if one of the arbitrators cannot obtain permission for travel into Saudi Arabia for a hearing?
a. The institution should replace the arbitrators with ones who are able to obtain visas for travel to Saudi Arabia.
b. The arbitrators should hold the hearing outside of Saudi Arabia.
c. The arbitration can simply be concluded without any hearing taking place, so there is no need for the arbitrators to travel.

3.8 Big Cities vs. Small Cities

While a party may want to secure a 'home court advantage' by insisting on arbitration in the city where it has its business operations, this can be a problem if the city is not recognized as common venue for international arbitration. It can be an even bigger problem if the chosen seat is also too small to have a large number of judges with experience handling large, international cases. It is advisable for *both* parties to select a city with an international reputation as a seat of arbitration.

> *Exercise 3.16: Intermediate*
> For a large contract to build a highway in Bulgaria, the New York engineering and construction company has sent the buyer a draft contract that provides for disputes to be resolved by arbitration. The proposed legal seat for the arbitration is Binghamton, New York. This is a city in northern New York state with approximately 50,000 inhabitants. If you are representing either of the parties, do you see any possible problems that might arise as a result of agreeing on a small city for the place of arbitration.

3.9 Institutional vs. *Ad Hoc* Arbitration

Arbitration comes in two general forms: one is administered by an arbitration institution ('institutional' arbitration) and the other is not administered by an institution ('ad hoc' arbitration). Parties drafting arbitration agreements for international contracts should always specify whether the arbitration will be administered by an institution or, if not, which rules of *ad hoc* arbitration procedure should apply.

> *Exercise 3.17: Intermediate*
> Since institutions 'administer' arbitrations, can you think of any differences that are likely to exist between how an arbitration is started and notified in cases administered by institutions vs. *ad hoc* proceedings?

CHAPTER 3 NEGOTIATING METHODS OF DISPUTE RESOLUTION

Exercise 3.18: Advanced
The parties, one from Japan and the other from Peru, are in an advanced stage of negotiations and would like you to draft a multi-tier clause. They do not expect there to be any disputes, they say, so in case of any disagreements, they want a written notice to be sent to the other party for their senior executives to attempt to resolve the dispute amicably through negotiation, failing which the dispute would be referred to arbitration to be completed under the UNCITRAL Arbitration Rules within 90 days. Which of the below elements of the clause could benefit from more details?
a. Negotiation
b. UNCITRAL Arbitration Rules
c. 90 days for completion

3.10   Choosing among Different Arbitration Institutions

There are many good options among the leading global, regional and national arbitration institutions, with rules and practices that are similar, although the fees they charge are often calculated in different ways. At the same time, there are also arbitration institutions – especially at a local or national level – that do not have a good reputation either for conducting international arbitrations (although they may be capable of handling domestic arbitrations) or that may not have a particularly strong reputation even in the region where they are headquartered. For example, there are institutions that exist only in name even though they have never provided any actual service of arbitration, and there are even institutions that are organized with the purpose of obtaining arbitration appointments for a small cabal of local lawyers and which cannot be trusted to ensure that the procedure leads to a competent or neutral arbitration award.[76]

The issue that therefore comes up, with some frequency in international contract negotiations, is whether to accept or insist upon a particular institution, or type of institution. In other words, how does one know whether a particular arbitration is reliable?

An entire separate volume could be dedicated to this issue and the difference of the world's many arbitration institutions. A short answer, however, is that parties opting for international arbitration should select one of the leading global or regional institutions to administer any disputes that arise out of their contract. A shortlist of the leading global institutions would include without question the ICC, LCIA, SIAC, HKIAC and the AAA/ICDR. A shortlist of leading regional institutions would be much longer.

Which institution a party should recommend (or accept if the other side insists upon their choice) will likely depend on the centre of gravity of the dispute: for example, if both parties are from Asia, an Asian institution or one of the global institutions would make more sense than, say, a regional institution such as the

---

76   *See, e.g. id.*, pp. 1-134-36.

CHAPTER 3 NEGOTIATING METHODS OF DISPUTE RESOLUTION

DIS in Germany (even though the DIS unquestionably possesses the skills to capably administer an Asian arbitration). If the parties are from different parts of the world, leverage may allow one party to insist on an institution nearer to home; if not, one of the global institutions is likely to be an acceptable choice to all parties.

But what can a party do if the other side insists on the name of an institution and information about it is difficult to obtain? While an institution's rules and how it charges fees are certainly important when comparing different institutions, there are some even more basic considerations to help a lawyer determine whether an unfamiliar institution is acceptable or is a genuine 'deal-breaker' for the proposed contract.[77]

– **Governance information:** Does the institution provide the names and relevant information about its leaders and/or its arbitration court on an easily accessible website? Information about who runs an institution will say much about its competency, international capability and impartiality. If an opposing party proposes an unfamiliar institution that is not transparent about its leadership, that should be treated as a red flag regarding the institution's reliability and independence.
– **List of arbitrators:** If the institution publishes a list of arbitrators who have registered to conduct arbitrations under its rules (and many do), an obvious question is whether the names appear to be a fraternity of local lawyers or a modern, diverse of names from different countries.
– **Number of arbitrations and international arbitrations the institution has conducted in each of the past three years:** Reliable institutions track and publish this type of information. For an international arbitration, parties can legitimately ask if the institution has experience administering cases with parties from different countries and, if so, how much experience.
– **Methods of arbitrator appointment or replacement:** Institutions should not be ashamed to disclose how, in the absence of agreement of the parties, they appoint or replace arbitrators. Is this by a formal consultative process with a court or committee of professionals, or a decision made by a single individual in the organization (which would be a cause for concern)? It would be a serious red flag if the institution cannot explain how it carries out this most fundamental function of arbitration.

Exercise 3.19: Basic
In an international contract negotiation, you represent the seller. The buyer is based in the Grand Duchy of Fenwick and is insisting that the contract require disputes to be resolved by the arbitration under the Arbitration Rules of the Court of Arbitration of the Chamber of Commerce of the Grand Duchy of Fenwick. Neither

---

[77] *See* T. Garcia-Reyes & M. Mcilwrath, 'Arbitration Institutions: Five Things Your Website Must Do to Attract Cases', available at http://arbitrationblog.kluwerarbitration.com/2018/01/17/mike/ 2017.

you nor your colleagues have heard of this institution, and it appears to have no website with its rules or organization. The best you have found is a website of the Grand Duchy Chamber of Commerce, which says that the Chamber assists with tourism and wine exportation, and provides arbitration services.

The site gives only a phone number for arbitration services, which you called to ask for information. The president of the institution himself answered your call. He lamented that the government had not provided sufficient funds to develop a website but that the institution is in fact a very serious one. When you asked about how they appoint arbitrators, he said that his reputation in the Grand Duchy for neutrality and competence in arbitration is known to everyone and that he only appoints arbitrators who have become 'close personal friends' after years of working in arbitrations together or who are recommended to him by counsel he respects. He tells you not to worry, that you can accept his institution's rules of arbitration with confidence that you will have a very good arbitration if there is ever any dispute.

You do not feel very confident with this institution at all. But your client is very concerned that if they do not accept it, the buyer will find another seller.

1. Set out your concerns about this institution and what you see as the risks to your client if they accept the contract with this arbitration institution.
2. Draft talking points for your upcoming negotiation with the buyer's lawyer, setting out reasons for why this institution is not acceptable to your client, your counterproposal(s) (this can be one or more options), and reasons supporting your counterproposal(s).

Exercise 3.20: Basic

In the same example as before, the buyer in the Grand Duchy of Fenwick has agreed to a global international institution instead of the one it was proposing from its country's chamber of commerce. You have done such a good job convincing your client of the importance of a reliable institution that the client has done their own research and has now decided that they must have the ICC Arbitration Rules. The buyer is insisting on SIAC Arbitration Rules. The place of arbitration is agreed to be in the capital of the Grand Duchy of Fenwick, a location at which neither the ICC nor SIAC have any offices. What should you advise your client?

a. The ICC and SIAC are both good institutions with an international reputation. Each regularly administer arbitrations all around the world where neither institution has offices. Local counsel can be consulted as to whether there is any idiosyncratic law of the Grand Duchy of Fenwick requiring an arbitration institution to be physically present in the country in order for its awards to be enforceable in the Grand Duchy, but it is unlikely to be the case.
b. Neither the ICC nor SIAC can be selected because they do not have any offices in the Grand Duchy of Fenwick.
c. If the client wants to walk away from the contract because the buyer refuses to accept the ICC, that is for the client to decide, not the lawyer, and you should not give the client any reasons that might change their mind.

CHAPTER 3 NEGOTIATING METHODS OF DISPUTE RESOLUTION

3.11 Arbitration vs. Courts: Different Ways of Approaching the Law

Exercise 3.21: Intermediate
The parties are renewing a contract for the sale of petroleum products produced at the seller's refinery in Thailand. Their old contract previously provided for the courts of Thailand, the seller's principal place of business, to resolve any disputes. Fortunately, there have not been any disputes. In this new contract, they are planning to include an arbitration clause instead of the courts. In this case, which of the following factors would you consider most critical *only* with respect to the enforceability of the arbitration clause and any arbitration awards rendered?
1. Conflict of laws rules typically applied by courts in Thailand and New Zealand.
2. Thailand's and New Zealand's environmental laws.
3. *Ad hoc* vs. institutional arbitration.
4. If institutional, whether there are any international arbitration institutions in Thailand or New Zealand that can administer an arbitration.
5. Ratification of the United Nations Convention on the Recognition and Enforcement of Foreign Arbitral Awards (The 1958 New York Convention) by Thailand or New Zealand.
6. The range of potential seats of the arbitration, including whether the courts and national laws of Thailand and New Zealand will enforce agreements to arbitrate, before considering a seat in either country.

Group Exercise 3.22: Intermediate
The facts are the same as those in the exercise above regarding the sale of refined petroleum products from Thailand to New Zealand, and the parties have agreed in principle to include an arbitration clause. In addition, they have also agreed that their contract will be governed by the substantive laws of Thailand. But they would like to know if their choice of arbitration – instead of Thai courts – will affect the application of Thai law. It was one thing for a Thai judge to apply Thai law, but now it could be arbitrators who have no training in Thai law at all.

3.12 Arbitration vs. Courts: Offensive vs. Defensive Strategies

Exercise 3.23: Basic
The seller manufactures locomotives for railroads and provides ancillary services for operating and maintaining them. The seller is currently negotiating a contract for the supply of railroad engine maintenance services to a railroad network operated by the buyer in its home country, the Grand Duchy of Fenwick.
The buyer is a family-owned business that has been granted the railways concession by the Grand Duchy government. The seller has proposed arbitration, and the buyer has refused, explaining that its government concession requires all supply contracts to be governed by Grand Duchy law with disputes referred to the Grand Duchy's courts. The jurisdiction of the courts is a condition that must be accepted or the seller will not be awarded the contract. Grand Duchy commercial law was virtually a

cut and pasted from the modern German law of obligations, and your client has no difficulty accepting it. The courts are a different matter. According to Transparency International, the Grand Duchy's courts are not regarded as neutral and parties frequently complain about corruption.

Which of the following considerations might be relevant to the question of whether your client can accept the contract with the Grand Duchy courts, assuming that your client's greatest concern is the certainty of being paid for work performed under the contract?

a. The fact that the buyer likely has all of its assets only in the Grand Duchy of Fenwick, and therefore a local court judgment will be as enforceable (or even more enforceable) against the buyer's assets than an international arbitration award rendered in a different country.
b. The fact that the contract is one for providing services, and if the buyer does not promptly pay, then the seller can limit its exposure by suspending or terminating those services before a large debt is created for the buyer.
c. The chance that the seller might be able to propose in another part of the contract methods of financial guaranty or security, such as a letter of credit or even advance payments, in order to avoid a situation in which the seller must rely on a court action to obtain compensation.
d. The fact that the seller is providing a particular technology that the buyer needs, and which may not be readily available on the market, giving the seller some leverage to obtain payment in the event of buyer's default, without resorting to the courts. (In other words, if the seller suspends its maintenance services because the buyer is not paying, then the buyer's railroad may not continue to operate for very long.)
e. All of the above.

Exercise 3.24: Basic

Following further negotiations, the parties have now agreed on a draft arbitration clause. Which of these dispute resolution provisions could pose a problem for them?

a. Arbitration administered by the Cairo Regional International Center for International Commercial Arbitration (CRCICA) and seated in Cairo.
b. UNCITRAL arbitration rules administered by the London Court of International Arbitration (LCIA) and seated in Tripoli.
c. Arbitration administered by the Federation of Oils, Seeds and Fats Associations Ltd (FOSFA) and seated in London.
d. Arbitration administered by the London Maritime Arbitrators Association (LMAA) and seated in London.

Discuss.

> *Exercise 3.25: Intermediate*
> The parties have discussed further and consider that an arbitration seated in Africa is the best compromise in the circumstances but are conscious about costs and time to resolve this dispute. What would be your main concerns as a result?
> Research and discuss.

> *Exercise 3.26: Intermediate*
> Assume that the parties have agreed to include an arbitration clause under the rules and administered by, CRCICA, sole arbitrator, and seated in N'Djamena. You have been informed that the seller has trading partners and possible assets in Khartoum (Sudan), Bamako (Mali) and Mogadishu (Somalia). As counsel for the buyer, devise a strategy plan to enforce a potential favourable arbitral award.

3.13 Agreements to Mediate before Arbitration or Court Litigation

Many parties begin their dispute resolution clause by stating that the parties 'shall attempt to resolve their dispute first by negotiation'. While this language may seem pleasing to the commercial (non-lawyer) stakeholders in the negotiation, there is little real value in such clauses. Negotiation is always an option that is usually attempted before the parties resort to arbitration or court litigation. Making this good intention a contractual requirement is unlikely to result in more negotiating than already taking place.

By contrast, a requirement to mediate is more likely to bring the parties together in a way that will result in the intended effect of generating a settlement.

A dispute resolution clause that contains mediation before a requirement to submit disputes to court or arbitration is known as a 'step' or 'tiered' clause, because the procedures are sequenced. The parties start with a non-binding process, mediation, and if they do not settle will end with a binding process, arbitration or litigation.

Requiring mediation can also be considered a means of mitigating concerns about the method of dispute resolution that the parties will include. That is, if the parties are more likely to settle their dispute before proceeding to the binding form of resolution, then an imperfect form of binding resolution is less likely to be activated.

> *Exercise 3.27: Basic*
> Alexis is representing a company that supplies logistics services and is in negotiations with a customer in Port Harcourt, Nigeria. The potential customer has insisted that the contractual form of dispute resolution should be arbitration in Port Harcourt, and this is non-negotiable if Alexis' client wants to close the contract.
> Discuss some of the things that Alexis might propose to mitigate his concerns over Port Harcourt as a place of arbitration.

3.14 Further Practice in Dispute Resolution

Exercise 3.28: Basic
This is a negotiation of a contract between a seller in Dubai (United Arab Emirates) and a buyer in Singapore for the sale of gold to be shipped from the port of Sohar (Oman) and paid in two instalments (at the time of shipping and at the time of receipt of the goods).
If the buyer defaults on payment, where should the seller file a legal action to get paid?
a. The judicial courts in Dubai
b. The judicial courts in Singapore
c. The judicial courts in Sohar

Exercise 3.29: Intermediate
With the same facts as the exercise above: Shortly after paying the first instalment, the buyer filed a court action in the courts of Singapore seeking a court order to prevent the seller from delivering the goods. Assuming the seller wishes the buyer to take delivery, which court should the seller take action or respond?

Exercise 3.30: Basic
Negotiation of contract between a buyer in Rotterdam, Netherlands, and a seller in San José (Costa Rica) for the sale of bananas. The contract provides for Dutch law and Dutch courts. If the buyer defaults payment, where should the seller file a legal action?
a. Courts of Rotterdam
b. Courts of San José

Exercise 3.31: Basic
Consider the case scenario above. If the seller does not deliver the goods, where should the buyer file a legal action?
a. Courts of San José
b. Courts of Rotterdam

Notes

Chapter 4 Defective Choice of Law and Dispute Resolution Clauses – Prevention and Management of Potential Risks

> **Learning Objectives**
> – Prevention: avoiding defective clauses in the first place
> – Management: mitigating the effects of defective choice of law and dispute resolution clauses

A poorly drafted choice of law or dispute resolution clause is something to be avoided. Any defects may put the implementation of the parties' real intentions at risk. Such clauses are known as 'pathological clauses'.[78] They typically lack a required element or contain excessive terms or verbiage that makes the clause inoperative or undermines its purpose.

For example, as discussed in Chapter 3, the heart of an arbitration agreement is to refer disputes to arbitration, thereby excluding the jurisdiction of the courts. To achieve this is relatively easy. Let us say that a dispute resolution clause states that "all disputes shall be resolved by arbitration in London". While this lacks some important details such as the rules of arbitration to be applied, the clause is not pathological. One might ask, what does this clause provide for? An *ad hoc* arbitration conducted under English procedural law, an arbitration conducted under the rules of a 'London'-based institution such as the LCIA (the London Court of International Arbitration) or some other type of arbitration seated in London?

---

78 *See* more in Benjamin G. Davis, 'Pathological Clauses: Frédéric Eisemann's Still Vital Criteria', *Arbitration International*, Volume 7, Issue 4, 1 December 1991, pp. 365-388.

These are relevant questions of how the arbitration will be conducted, and if the parties are unable to agree on them once a dispute arises, then the answers will be provided by a court in London. But the simple language effectively accomplishes its straightforward goal: arbitration will be the means by which disputes will be decided.

Now consider the same example, only with some additional language, "all disputes shall be resolved either by arbitration or in the courts of London". This clause does not exclude the jurisdiction of the courts and it does not set out any criteria by which arbitration should be employed by the parties. Suppose that one party initiates an LCIA arbitration on the basis of this language while the other party files a similar suit in the London commercial court. Unless the party that filed in court expressly consents to having the dispute decided in the arbitration (and to continue with the London court proceeding), the LCIA may well reject the request, since the institution has not been specified, the clause does not exclude the jurisdiction of the courts, and a court proceeding is already underway in London in which the issue of arbitrability would be determined. In the (unlikely) event that an arbitral institution in this situation permits the arbitration to proceed in the absence of the court's determination or the parties' consent, and a tribunal is put in place, any subsequent arbitration award may be subject to challenge by a reviewing court should it find that the arbitration clause was null and void.

Defects are typically diagnosed in the following scenarios: (i) lack of evidence of the parties' clear intention to arbitrate the dispute or the binding nature of the arbitration (e.g. may vs. shall); (ii) lack of clarity whether other forms of dispute resolution have been agreed or a conflicting dispute resolution provision calling for both courts and arbitration; (iii) an inaccurate or impossible-to-implement designation of an arbitral institution or the applicable rules (or designation of non-existent institutions or rules).

The possibility of a defect increases when there are integrated dispute resolution mechanisms, such as those that include issues of joinder of additional parties or multi-tier dispute resolution clauses.[79] An ambiguous arbitration clause could

---

79 See more in Klaus Peter Berger, 'Law and Practice of Escalation Clauses', *Journal of the London Court of International Arbitration*, Vol. 22, Issue 1, 2006, pp. 1-17; James H. Carter, 'Issues Arising from Integrated Dispute Resolution Clauses', *in* Albert Jan Van den Berg (Ed.), *New Horizons in International Commercial Arbitration and Beyond – ICCA International Arbitration Congress*, Kluwer Law International, Hague, 2005, pp. 446-469; ICC case nos. 4230, 6276, 7422 and 6277; *Tribunal Federal Suíço – 6 de junho de 2007 – X. Ltda v. Y.; and* ICC International Court of Arbitration Bulletin, Vol. 14, Issue 1, 2003; *Channel Tunnel – Channel Tunel Group Ltd. (UK) and France Manche S.A (Fr) v. Balfour Beatty Construction Ltd. (UK)* et al, 1992; *Cable & Wireless Plc v. IBM United Kingdom Ltd.* (2003); *Poiré v. Tripier* (2003); *Peyrin v. Société Polyclinique des Fleurs* (2000); Doug Jones, 'Dealing with Multi-tiered Dispute Resolution Process', *The International Journal of Arbitration, Mediation and Dispute Management*, Vol. 75, Issue 2, May 2009, pp. 188-198; and Alexander Jolles,

therefore trigger a legitimate jurisdictional challenge and resulting delays (and costs[80]) given the legal issues pertaining to the validity or interpretation of the arbitration clause or the enforceability of an award.

Take the example of this dispute resolution clause: "If a dispute arises, the parties agree to submit to arbitration in Milan, but in case of litigation, the Tribunal of Milan shall have exclusive jurisdiction." How can this clause be put into operation? If either party objects to the jurisdiction of the arbitrators or the courts, the question of which must decide the merits of the dispute must first be decided by a Milan court. But even before the parties reach that point, how can they negotiate an effective resolution of any dispute without knowing the means by which their contractual rights and obligations will be enforced?

Choice of law provisions can also suffer from defects in drafting, such as these real-life examples: "the rules and principles applied by the majority of national legal systems" or "the law most commonly applied in the energy sector". Paraphrasing our question above, how would a judge or arbitrator understand and apply the parties' intentions?

There are only two avenues available to parties when a dispute arises and the language of their arbitration or choice of law agreements is defective: (i) agreement to amend the clause(s) and/or agree to submit the dispute to arbitration (a 'submission agreement'); or (ii) initiate court proceedings for the clause to be amended, presenting evidence that the parties intended a given law or jurisdiction. The first option is obviously only available in the rare case in which disputing parties are able to reach an agreement on such an important issue as the choice of forum or law. The second may leave substantial uncertainty until the court provides its ruling.

Thus, the greater question should be, how to avoid defects from happening in the first place? The short answer is to employ simple language and wherever possible adopt the model clauses provided by arbitral institutions. While customized clauses may be very attractive to businesses inasmuch as they can address a myriad of scenarios – and ultimately parties like to be in control – these clauses are often costly due to learning and implementation costs.[81] In addition, standard or model clauses have the benefit of being 'bullet-proof', so why not use them?

Consider a negotiation between a Uruguayan seller and a Chinese buyer for the sale of frozen bovine meat. The draft dispute resolution clause reads as follows:

'Consequences of Multi-tier Arbitration Clause: Issues of Enforcement', *Arbitration*, Vol. 72, 2006, pp. 329-338; Michael Pryles, 'Multi-tiered Dispute Resolution Clause', *Journal of International Arbitration*, Vol. 18, 2001, pp. 159-176; and Peter M. Wolrich, 'Multi-tiered Clauses: ICC Perspectives in Light of the New ICC ADR Rules', Special Supplement to *ICC International Court of Arbitration Bulletin*, 2001, pp. 7-22.

80 *See* G. Moser, *supra* note 1, pp. 134-140.
81 *Id.*, pp. 138-139.

"Arbitration, if any, by Swiss Rules in Geneva". What would be your main legal preoccupations regarding this clause?

This draft clause poses a number of legal issues meriting concern: there is no clear reference to the arbitration rules which will govern the arbitration (Swiss Rules is a rather unclear choice!); the reference to 'Geneva' is also unclear as to whether it refers to the legal seat or the place of the hearings and there is no arbitral institution to administer the case – which is not a critical issue per se given that *ad hoc* arbitration is also an option; however, the consequences of having an institutional arbitration and an *ad hoc* one should also be factored in.

Following the scenario above, assume that the parties decided to leave the clause as drafted and the Uruguayan seller now wishes to initiate arbitration proceedings. Which of these considerations in the dispute resolution clause could pose a threat to the seller's intentions?

a. The indeterminacy of 'if any'.
b. The lack of an agreed set of rules or administering institution.
c. The lack of a designated seat of the arbitration.

While the parties appear to have designated the seat, they have been unnecessarily vague as to the choice of rules and institution. What would be your next course of action?

The best – and perhaps most intuitive – course would be for the parties to agree to vary the clause with a view to providing for a set of rules to govern the arbitration and, preferably, an arbitral institution to administer the case. If no such course is envisaged, the next best action would be for the Uruguayan seller to initiate court proceedings in Geneva, presenting evidence that the parties intended a given set of rules and (if any) an institution to administer the arbitration. In the event that the party is unable to present evidence, or the matter becomes more contentious (i.e. the Chinese buyer objects to the Uruguayan seller's proposal), the Uruguayan party might instead wish to seek the court's assistance with selecting a suitable set of rules and (if any) an institution to administer the case.

Assume the same factual background above. The choice of law provision reads as follows: "Choice of law: any disputes which might arise would be settled on the basis of Anglo-Saxon principles of law."

Which of these considerations in the choice of law provision are most worrying?

a. Principles of law
b. Anglo-Saxon
c. Absence of a state law

All three are problematic. Perhaps by 'Anglo-Saxon principles of law', the parties meant the principles akin to English law or common law countries more generally, but a judge or arbitrator tasked with determining what this means may conclude that it means nothing at all. The arbitrators (or judge) may then be required to determine that a particular law will apply in its place. Arbitrators will typically be guided by the arbitration rules applicable, and they may also refer to the legal framework of the seat in this case.

Obviously, the sensible lawyer will wish to avoid the uncertainty that may arise and will seek to convince an opposing negotiator to adopt language that is clear and that does not give rise to disputes over how the disputes should be decided.

Exercises: Preventing and Mitigating the Effects of Defective Choice of Law and Dispute Resolution Clauses

This section sets out several exercises based on the discussion points of this chapter. They are both preventive and corrective in nature and are aimed at assisting you in identifying and managing the effects of defective clauses more efficiently. These exercises provide further guidance on how to avoid being caught up by defective clause in the first place.

> *Exercise 4.1: Basic*
> Negotiation between a Bordeaux (France) seller and a Calgary (Alberta province, Canada) buyer for the sale of 100,000 bottles of red wine. The dispute resolution clause reads as follows:
>
> Any dispute arising under or relating to this Agreement shall be finally settled according to the procedures of this article. In case of arbitration, the LCIA Rules of Arbitration 1996 shall apply, in Paris; in case of litigation, any dispute shall be brought before the courts of Calgary.
>
> Considering that the LCIA Rules of Arbitration do not have a 1996 version, in what ways could this clause be considered potentially 'pathological' for one or both parties (more than one may apply)?
> a.   Referring to the LCIA Rules of Arbitration 1996.
> b.   The reference to Paris.
> c.   Referring disputes to both arbitration and litigation in the courts.
> d.   The phrase, "Any dispute arising under or relating to this Agreement".
>
> *Exercise 4.2: Advanced*
> Assuming that in the same contract negotiation between the French seller and the Canadian buyer, the parties agreed the following choice of law clause: "*rules and principles applied by the majority of national legal systems*". Assuming the parties are able to get their dispute before a validly constituted arbitral tribunal and you have been appointed the chair of that tribunal, how would you address this? Going into your case management conference with the parties, what questions might you ask them to agree or address in their submissions in order for you to determine their dispute?

Exercise 4.3: Intermediate

Assume the same factual elements of exercise above, but that the parties (from France and Canada) also specified that "this contract shall be governed by the rules and principles applicable to the international wine industry instead of the United Nations Convention on the International Sale of Goods" and nothing else about choice of law.

A dispute has arisen between the parties after delivery of the wine. The Canadian buyer protests that the French seller delivered bottles that are each 650 ml in size when the expectation was for the delivery of 750-ml bottles. The buyer says 750 ml is the 'standard' definition of a wine bottle, even if 'standard' is not a contract term, and the parties' contract says nothing about the size of the bottles.

The seller says that it has never sold 750-ml bottles of wine and that the buyer should have known that it would receive only 650-ml bottles.

Assume that, despite the lack of clarity in their drafting, an LCIA arbitration is validly underway. You are the sole arbitrator who has been appointed to decide this dispute. You are preparing for the 'case management conference', which is an initial meeting with the parties to establish the procedure for the arbitration and a timetable.

The laws of Alberta and France both offer straightforward ways to resolve contractual ambiguity, but they are not the same. The CISG is a body of law that could have helped, but the parties have expressly excluded its application.

a. What questions might you pose to the parties to help you determine whether the seller met its contractual obligation by delivering 650-ml bottles of wine or is in breach of the contract?
b. What might you add to the parties' choice of law clause in order to make it easier for the arbitrator to decide contractual ambiguities?
c. What might you delete from the parties' choice of law clause in order to make it easier for the arbitrator to decide contractual ambiguities?

Exercise 4.4: Intermediate

A negotiation is underway between a seller in Alicante (Spain) and a buyer in Ankara (Turkey) for the sale of salted fish. Their draft contract provides for UNCITRAL Arbitration Rules and its choice of law clause reads as follows: "This Agreement shall be governed in accordance with the private international law".

As a party advisor, do you expect any difficulty with the proposed choice of law clause if you must enforce the contract on behalf of the buyer or the seller? Please draft an assessment of the legal risks that parties may encounter if they decide to adopt such a clause.

Variation: Assume the same scenario as above. You represent the Spanish seller. The Turkish buyer has given further consideration to the negotiations and has proposed that the parties adopt the following options in the place of the UNCITRAL arbitration rules and 'private international law'.

a) "The Agreement shall be governed by the laws of the International Chamber of Commerce (ICC) for any disputes arising hereunder."
b) "This Agreement and any dispute or claim arising out of or in connections with it, its subject matter, validity, or enforcement shall be governed by and construed in accordance with the laws of Spain or Turkey."

Can you propose better options for the parties, and what arguments might help you convince the Turkish party to adopt them?

Exercise 4.5: Basic

You are the counsel for a Liverpool, United Kingdom (UK) buyer in negotiations with a seller in Mexico City (Mexico) for the sale of broadcasting equipment. Your client, the buyer, has asked you to insist that the final contract include the following choice of law clause: "the governing law of this contract shall be the material law (both statutory and common law) of the United Kingdom".

Variation 1: Before you propose this language to the Spanish seller, are there any recommendations you would make to your client to improve the clause?

Variation 2: Assume that your UK client has instead insisted on including the following language: "the governing law of this contract shall be the laws of the courts of the UK, without regard to any conflict of laws rules". What is the most troublesome part of the clause?
a. Laws of the courts of the UK
b. Conflict of laws rules
c. Both (a) and (b)

Variation 3: Assume that the parties have expressed their preference for the laws of England and Wales to apply but want to ensure that this choice would not attract any other laws at all. How would you draft such clause?

Exercise 4.6: Basic

Negotiation between a Brazilian seller and a Chinese buyer for the sale of soybeans. The choice of dispute resolution clause read as follows: "[a] Any disputes arising out of the contract shall be resolved by arbitration, [b] to be carried out by arbitrators designated by the International Chamber of Commerce [c] in Paris [d] in accordance with the arbitration procedure set forth in the Brazilian Code of Civil Procedure, [e] with due regard for the law of the place of arbitration in Paris, France".
a. If you could only delete one portion of this clause, [a] to [e], which one would you delete?
b. If you cannot change any part of the clause, what problem[s] do you think might be encountered when putting this clause into operation? Can you think of any ways to reduce or overcome these problems?

Exercise 4.7: Basic

Negotiation between a Swedish seller and an Austrian buyer of technical consulting services. The choice of dispute resolution clause reads as follows: "Disputes shall be subject to arbitration and shall be referred to three arbitrators. [Party A] will appoint one arbitrator and [Party B] will designate another one. Said arbitrators will appoint a third, presiding, arbitrator by mutual agreement. If the arbitrators designated by [Party A] and [Party B] fail to reach an agreement on the appointment of the presiding arbitrator, it shall be designated by [Party B] from a list of five arbitrators proposed by [Party A] from the Official List of Arbitrators of the International Court of Arbitration of the Chamber of Commerce (ICC)".

It is known that the ICC does not keep any 'Official List' of arbitrators or any list that is publicly available. After each item below, identify circumstances that could pose a threat to a party's ability to quickly initiate an arbitration in the face of an opposing party that is seeking to delay the arbitration.

Problem areas:

a. The lack of an appointing authority. Potential problem that could arise: *Example: Party A refuses to propose a list of arbitrators for Party B to consider, and there is no reference to what authority should resolve this lack of action by Party A.*
b. The lack of agreed rules of arbitration. Potential problem that could arise:
c. The lack of a designated seat of the arbitration. Potential problem that could arise:
d. The reference to an 'Official List' from the ICC. Potential problem that could arise:

Exercise 4.8: Basic

Re-write the above clause between the Swedish and Austrian parties so that it is not pathological and validly adopts the ICC Rules of Arbitration and provides for three arbitrators.

Exercise 4.9: Advanced

A contract between a Bulgarian seller and an Indian buyer of accounting services provides for the following method of resolving disputes:

Any disputes under this Agreement shall be amicably settled by mediation. If the dispute is not settled within 30 days of commencement of mediation, it shall be resolved by arbitration under the Arbitration and Conciliation Act 1996 of India, before a tribunal of three arbitrators appointed in accordance with the Act, with one arbitrator appointed by each party and the third appointed by the co-arbitrators. The place of arbitration shall be Delhi, India, and the law governing the Agreement shall be the laws of India.

The Arbitration and Conciliation Act, 1996,[82] draws on the UNCITRAL model arbitration law, with some departures. The 1996 Act does not mention 'mediation' but does refer to the practice of 'conciliation', which, depending on the country, can be the same as mediation or a different practice. As to the 'commencement' of conciliation, the 1996 Act says the following:

62. Commencement of conciliation proceedings.
(1) The party initiating conciliation shall send to the other party a written invitation to conciliate under this Part, briefly identifying the subject of the dispute.
(2) Conciliation proceedings shall commence when the other party accepts in writing the invitation to conciliate.
(3) If the other party rejects the invitation, there will be no conciliation proceedings.
(4) If the party initiating conciliation does not receive a reply within thirty days from the date on which he sends the invitation, or within such other period of time as specified in the invitation, he may elect to treat this as a rejection of the invitation to conciliate and if he so elects, he shall inform in writing the other party accordingly.

A dispute has arisen and the seller wishes to initiate arbitration as quickly as possible to obtain payment but recognizes that there is an obligation to attempt to resolve the dispute by mediation first.
a. In the light of the contractual dispute resolution clause and the 1996 Act, draft a letter from the seller inviting the buyer to participate in a mediation. The letter should balance the buyer's need to secure a resolution as quickly as possible with the need to demonstrate compliance with the contractual dispute resolution clause. The letter should also address the gap left by the dispute clause by failing to refer to any rules of mediation or process for appointing a mediator. Assume that the buyer will reject the mediation request or will fail to respond and that the letter will become evidence in the arbitration to defeat the buyer's objections that the seller did not comply with the contractual dispute methods.
b. Revise the Parties' dispute resolution clause to preserve the requirement of mediation and also arbitration under the Indian Arbitration & Conciliation Act of 1996, but eliminating the problems arising from the undefined mediation requirement.

Exercise 4.10: Advanced
With reference to the agreement in Exercise 4.9, between a Bulgarian seller and an Indian buyer of accounting services, assume that the parties have made it past the undefined mediation phase and you are about to embark on arbitration under the Indian Arbitration and Conciliation Act of 1996. The Act refers repeatedly to

---

82   Full text available at www.indiacode.nic.in/handle/123456789/1978?sam_handle=123 456789/1362.

'international commercial arbitration', and it appears clear that your dispute qualifies as one since your client is Bulgarian, a non-Indian party.

Section 11 of the 1996 Act[83] provides the procedures for appointing arbitrators:

11. Appointment of arbitrators.
(1) A person of any nationality may be an arbitrator, unless otherwise agreed by the parties.
(2) Subject to sub-section (6), the parties are free to agree on a procedure for appointing the arbitrator or arbitrators.
(3) Failing any agreement referred to in sub-section (2), in an arbitration with three arbitrators, each party shall appoint one arbitrator, and the two appointed arbitrators shall appoint the third arbitrator who shall act as the presiding arbitrator.
(4) If the appointment procedure in sub-section (3) applies and – (a) a party fails to appoint an arbitrator within thirty days from the receipt of a request to do so from the other party; or (b) the two appointed arbitrators fail to agree on the third arbitrator within thirty days from the date of their appointment, the appointment shall be made, upon request of a party, by 1 [the Supreme Court or, as the case may be, the High Court or any person or institution designated by such Court];
(5) *etc.*

Since your client will be the claimant party, you will be the first to nominate an arbitrator, and under the 1996 Act you are free to choose an arbitrator from any country, not just from India.

   a. Your client, the Bulgarian seller, has sent you an email posing the following problem for which they would like your advice: "We understand that there are no major legal issues in dispute with the buyer, and the only question is whether our services were rendered in accordance with international standards for services of the type provided under our contract. If so, then payment is due. We want to know whether we should appoint an arbitrator who is a retired Indian judge or if we should instead appoint a highly-regarded international arbitrator from outside of India who will be familiar with international standards and trade practices, and also international arbitration practices. Please write us a short memo setting out the "pros and cons" of appointing an Indian vs non-Indian arbitrator, and also identifying any concerns we should have if all three arbitrators are retired Indian judges or one or two are from outside of India."

   b. For their next contract in India, your Bulgarian client wants to be assured that if they have a dispute with the customer, two of the three arbitrators (the one they appoint and the chair) will be from outside India. There are two ways to do this: either by revising the above clause to expressly provide for different nationalities of arbitrators or choosing arbitration rules that expressly provide that the chair of the arbitral tribunal will not be of the same nationality as the

---

83 *Id.*

parties. Draft an arbitration agreement with the simplest solution you can propose that achieves your client's objective.

Notes

Chapter 5 Putting It All Together

> **Learning Objectives**
> – Negotiating dispute resolution and choice of law together
> – Factoring the subject matter of the contract into consideration
> – Risk vs. reward in accepting different forms of dispute resolution
> – How form of dispute resolution can influence interpretation of terms and conditions

In this chapter, we will explore the places where decisions on how to resolve disputes and what law to apply intersect with each other. Specifically, we look at how contracts are negotiated, with insights into how choice of law and dispute resolution relate to each other, to other terms and conditions of the contract, and to the subject matter of the contract and even the parties' relationship.

5.1 Group Negotiation and Discussion

Exercise 5.1: Basic
This exercise is a negotiation, which means it requires at least two participants. It works well either with one person on each side or groups of people. It requires one person or an instructor to allocate certain confidential information for each side, which is only the value that each side places on certain terms that they wish to negotiate for their choice of law and dispute resolution clauses. The instructions for creating the 'confidential information' are included in the Appendix and can be easily changed each time this exercise is used with a different group.

Negotiation Scenario
The scenario is a negotiation between, on the one side, the sales team of an international company based in London that sells highly engineered equipment for the energy and oil and gas industries and, on the other side, the purchasing team of a gas extraction and production company in Doha that is wholly owned by the state of Qatar. Both companies are fictional, but the background circumstances of oil and

gas fields are as real as the many international companies that supply technology and services from around the world to support their development and production.

The contract in question is the sale of three 'turbo-compressor units' for use in a liquefied natural gas (LNG) project in the Ras Laffan gas field in Qatar. Each unit includes gas turbines, compressors and auxiliary equipment.

The company that will produce LNG from the gas field is Ras Qatar Liquified (RQL). RQL has already selected the equipment supplier, International Multicorp (IM), after a review of the technology available on the market and IM's global reputation as a leading supplier of equipment for LNG.

This sort of equipment has an operational life of 20 to 30 years if it is operated and maintained properly. Over the course of the years, an owner of an oil or gas plant will often enter into additional contracts with the original equipment manufacturer for the supply of operation and maintenance services, as well as spares or replacement parts. While these ancillary agreements are valuable for the plant owner and provide for years of future profitability for the equipment supplier, they are not part of today's negotiation, which is focused on the very large contract for the supply of the equipment.

The contract will be very complex and contains at least 30 technical appendices, in addition to the main contract. The parties are still negotiating the commercial and technical terms. Although they have not yet agreed on a final price, $300 million is a reasonable estimate.

As for dispute resolution, both sides have agreed on arbitration, rather than the courts. Unfortunately, that is all they have agreed. They remain far apart on the form of arbitration and also the choice of law. If they cannot overcome these legal roadblocks, the contract negotiations will be terminated. Keep in mind that whatever is agreed today on choice of law and dispute resolution will probably also be adopted in any future contracts between RQL and IM.

Step 1: Assign Roles / Sides
Before negotiating, you should select sides or groups, with some individuals or groups representing International Multicorp on one side and the others representing Ras Qatar Liquified on the other.

Step 2: Define Your (Confidential) Negotiation Objectives
Below is a list of the dispute resolution and choice of law terms that need to be negotiated. You or your team should set the points that realistically would reflect each side's *preferences* for this contract. You allocate approximately 30 minutes to indicate the points, or weighting, based on what you think would be realistic for a company in your client's position.

These preferences are *confidential* information for your client (your side) only.

For example, if you represent Qatar in the negotiations, you may wish to consider whether the selection of Qatari law is important for a government-owned company, and therefore give it more points than other laws, or whether there may be a preference towards *ad hoc* arbitration rules based on perceptions of cost. Similarly, if you represent Multicorp, you may ask whether there are certain seats that a company based in London would prefer over the others or whether a company that does contracts around the world may have certain preferences for arbitration administered by global institutions.

Do not begin negotiating until you have established all of your objectives, i.e. given points to each category.

Since you will be seeking to obtain your preferences in the negotiation, you should be prepared to explain and defend the choices that you are advocating.

Step 3: Negotiate the Contract's Choice of Law and the Terms of the Arbitration Clause

Give yourselves approximately 30 minutes to negotiate all of the terms of the dispute resolution and choice of law clauses. You do not have to write the actual clauses, just negotiate the key terms below.

Senior management will assess the proposed contract based on how much risk it presents. A total of less than 12 points will be rejected. While 12-15 is not ideal, your management may accept it. Anything above 15 points will be viewed as a favourable result by the company.

Of course, management of both sides is also interested in how profitable or expensive the contract will be. Therefore, if the negotiation encounters any 'deal-breakers' (roadblocks), then the negotiators are authorized to trade price for improved contract terms. *The most either side can increase or reduce the final price is $5 million.*

Limitation on negotiation authority: As counsel, your ultimate goal is to protect your client from accepting a risk of open-ended (or unlimited) liability. Therefore, if you cannot succeed in negotiating at least 12 points, then you will need to inform Senior Management that the other side is insisting on terms that would make the entire contract so risky as to be unacceptable.

Step 4: Discuss the Results of the Negotiation

Total the points negotiated by your side (and the other side should do the same). Refer to the discussion notes contained in Appendix and allow at least 30 minutes to cover each of the points that you have negotiated. Feel free to share both your total points and your confidential rankings (negotiation objectives) with the other side.

Exercise 5.1 Scoring Form

Place of Arbitration

Rank the following from 6 to 1, with 6 being the *most desired* and 1 being the *least desired*. If there is a place that is especially troublesome, you can give it 0 points.	Doha __ points
	Dubai __ points

	London __ points
	Paris __ points
	Singapore __ points
	New York __ points

Arbitration Rules

Rank the following from 6 to 1, with 6 being the *most* desired and 1 being the *least* desired. If there is an institution that is especially troublesome, you can give it 0 points.	Cairo Regional Centre __ points
	HKIAC __ points
	ICC __ points
	ICDR __ points
	LCIA __ points
	Ad hoc/UNCITRAL __ points

Number of Arbitrators

Rank the following from 3 to 1, with 3 points being the *most desired* and 1 point being the *least desired*.	Sole arbitrator __ points
	Three arbitrators __ points
	Silence on number __ points

Mediation before Arbitration

Rank each of the following, with 4 points being the *most desired*, 2 points being *second most desired* and 0 points for the *least desired*.	Requirement to 'attempt mediation before arbitration' __ points
	Requirement to 'consider mediation before arbitration' __ points
	No requirement of mediation before arbitration __ points

Governing Law

Rank each of the following from 6 to 1, with 6 points being the *most desired* and 1 point being the *least desired*. If there is one law that is especially troublesome, you can give it 0 points.	English law __ points
	French law __ points
	New York law __ points

CHAPTER 5 PUTTING IT ALL TOGETHER

	Singapore law__ points
	Swiss law__ points
	Qatari law__ points
Time Limit on Duration of Arbitration	
Rank each of the following, with 2 points being the *most desired* and 0 points being the *least desired*.	No limit__ points
	12 months__ points
	6 months __ points
Language of Arbitration	
Rank each of the following, with 2 points being the *most desired* and 0 points being the *least desired*.	Arabic __ points
	English __ points
	Silence on language __ points

5.2 How Choice of Law and Dispute Resolution Can Alter Certain Contractual Terms

Certain terms in a contract can have very different meanings depending on what law is applied and also by the process that will be applied to resolve any disputes over that language.
Let us start simply with how the same contract term can have a radically different meaning, and impact on a contractual dispute, when the governing law is changed.

> *Exercise 5.2: Advanced*
> Swiss Machines is a company headquartered in Zurich that for several years has used standard terms and conditions of purchase drafted by the company's Swiss lawyers for all contracts with vendors.
> These standard terms and conditions contain a clause that provides for a 'penalty' for late delivery of goods or services. The clause states:
>
> 18.1. Penalty for Delay. In the event of any delay in delivery attributable to the Vendor, the Vendor shall pay the equivalent of 0.5% of the contract price per week of delay, up to a maximum or capped penalty of 10 weeks, or 5% of the total contract price. In addition to the penalty, Seller shall be entitled to recover any additional damages that it may demonstrate as arising from the Vendor's delay.

Assume that this clause is consistent with how Swiss law treats contractual penalty clauses and that it is valid and raises no surprising concerns under Swiss law. It is very different from a concept frequently encountered in common law jurisdictions, which is reflected in the long-standing concept that one may not 'penalize' a party in a contract and that 'liquidated damages' can only be compensatory in nature.

In a late-night negotiation with a key, strategic vendor in Birmingham, Swiss Machine's in-house counsel agreed to accept English law as the governing law of the contract, but the parties did not change Clause 18.1 which provides the penalty for delay. Under English law, even if a clause is labelled as 'penalty', it will be treated as a valid liquidated damages clause so long as it is a "genuine and not unconscionable pre-estimate of loss". Under English law, liquidated damages are considered full compensation (and a cap on liability) for the type of contractual losses for which they are specified. For example, where a contract provides for compensation in the form of an amount of liquidated damages for delay, a buyer cannot recover more than this contractually specified amount even if the delay caused much greater losses.

A dispute has arisen in which Swiss Machines has requested payment of the full 5% delay penalty plus $3 million in additional losses that it says were incurred in making alternative arrangements to overcome the delayed delivery. There is no dispute that the vendor was 10 weeks late in delivering. The only dispute is whether the 5% penalty is due and whether Swiss Machines can claim the additional $3 million in alleged losses caused by the delay.

1. Assume the parties agreed courts of Birmingham would resolve any disputes. How would an English judge approach the validity of the penalty clause? And how would the English judge likely treat Swiss Machine's request for $3 million of delay damages in addition to the full penalty?
2. Explain how a judge in Switzerland would handle the same issues if the parties had agreed that Swiss courts would resolve any contractual disputes.
3. Assume the parties agreed instead on arbitration and they appointed arbitrators from Germany, France and Italy, all countries that adopt a similar approach to contractual 'penalties' as Switzerland. How might they address the issue? Would it make any difference if some or even all of the arbitrators were from England, or from the United States and Canada (countries that adopt a similar approach to liquidated damages as England)?

Exercise 5.3: Intermediate

Assume the same facts as above, but the vendor now argues that the 5% contractual penalty is not due. The vendor's defence is that at the time of contracting, Swiss Machines had no valid reason to believe that any delay by the vendor would cause any damages. Swiss Machines says this does not matter because, in fact, it did incur losses of at least $3 million resulting from the delay.

Assuming that the contract language is the same as the 'penalty' provision in the previous exercise, which law will be more sympathetic to the vendor's argument, English or Swiss? Why?

5.3 Contractual Limitation of Liability and Choice of Law and Forum

The purpose of contractual limitation of liability clauses is to exclude certain types of damages from claims for losses or to cap the parties' liability at a certain amount. A common exclusion is liability for loss of profits resulting from a breach of the contract. The reason for this is that the party that would earn such profits is in a better position to predict and insure them.

While entire books are dedicated to discussing the qualification of damages under different legal systems, for the purposes of the exercises below we will make the following generalization for how this is accomplished in common law vs. civil law jurisdictions.

In jurisdictions like England and the United States (common law), parties will exclude liability for lost profits by referring to 'consequential damages' or 'indirect losses'. For example, if a vehicle transporting cargo breaks due to a defect in the engine, the direct damages would typically be the cost of repairing the vehicle. The consequential or indirect losses would be the profits that the company that owns or operates the vehicle did not earn as a result of the vehicle breaking down. In most instances, the parties' contract would provide a period of warranty of the seller's liability for the direct losses (the costs of repairs) but would exclude any liability of indirect/consequential damages (the lost profits).

In civil law jurisdictions, however, the direct/indirect distinction may not be drawn the same way as in the common law, or even exist at all. In Italy, for example, all losses that result from a breach of contract are 'direct'. The question for an Italian judge (applying Italian law) is whether it can be shown that the breaches caused the losses and whether such losses were reasonably foreseeable. For this reason, parties wishing to exclude liability for lost profits would typically phrase their exclusion to specifically do so, i.e. stating that the seller "shall not be liable for lost profits". Along the same lines, the parties will want to specifically name any other categories of damages that they wish to exclude from liability, such as loss of use or additional costs resulting from loss of use.

> ***Exercise 5.4: Basic***
> The parties have not yet agreed on the choice of law, but they have agreed on the contract's limitation of liability, which has been approved by their respective boards of directors after lengthy negotiations:
>
> "Notwithstanding anything to the contrary, Seller shall not be liable for claims for indirect or consequential loss of any nature of Buyer Group regardless of whether arising under contract, tort, or any other cause or action".
>
> Assume the limitation of liability is the most important contract clause for the seller, after price. If the buyer is unable or unwilling to change this clause, which law would be better suited to ensuring that the clause will effectively exclude the seller's liability for the buyer's lost profits damages in the event of a breach?

a. New York law (a common law jurisdiction)
b. French law (a civil law jurisdiction)

Exercise 5.5: Basic

Under the same facts as the preceding exercise, assume that the parties have agreed that the contract with the limitation of liability clause will be governed by French law (a civil law). The parties have also decided for disputes to be resolved by the courts of Paris.

If there is a dispute, which of the following damages might the court determine can be claimed (not excluded by the contractual limitation of liability)?

a. Lost profits resulting from a breach of the contract.
b. Additional costs incurred as a result of the contract not being performed during the breach.
c. Damages paid by the non-breaching party to its customers for delays in delivering to them as a result of the breach.
d. All of the above.

Exercise 5.6: Intermediate

Under the same facts as the preceding exercise, how would you revise the contract's limitation of liability clause to ensure that 'indirect' or 'consequential' losses, as contemplated by English or New York law, would be excluded by a French court? Would your language change if the parties decided to settle disputes instead through arbitration?

Exercise 5.7: Basic

A manufacturer in New York is negotiating a contract to sell industrial milling machines to a buyer in Paris. New York law provides an implied warranty against latent defects of 4 years from delivery of the goods and French law provides for 10 years from delivery. Under CISG Article 39(2), the warranty against latent defects would be two years from delivery, unless a longer or shorter period is stipulated in the contract. Both France and the United States have ratified the CISG.

The French buyer wants the contract to provide a warranty of 36 months plus an extended warranty for latent defects for an additional 24 months. In the negotiations, the New York seller has refused the additional, extended warranty against latent defects.

Which of these governing law provisions would allow the buyer to effectively overcome the seller's objection and obtain the right to claim against latent defects even if not provided in the contractual warranty?

1. New York law, expressly excluding the application of the CISG.
2. New York law, incorporating the CISG, Article 39(2).
3. French law, expressly excluding the application of the CISG.
4. French law, incorporating the CISG, Article 39(2)

CHAPTER 5 PUTTING IT ALL TOGETHER

Exercise 5.8: Basic

Assuming that in the same contract negotiation between a New York seller and a buyer in Paris, both parties wish the CISG to apply to their contract, which of these governing law provisions could pose a problem for them?
a. A clause that simply elects New York or French law as the governing law of the contract.
b. A clause that expressly specifies that the CISG shall apply.
c. A clause that specifies New York or French law and specifically that either the UCC (Uniform Commercial Code) or the French domestic law for the sale of goods shall apply.

Exercise 5.9: Basic

Assume that after lengthy negotiations, both parties have agreed on the following choice of law provision: "This contract shall be governed by the laws of France." As a compromise in negotiations, the seller also agreed to provide a full warranty, including for latent defects, of four years.

Seven years after delivery, the machine has stopped operating. The buyer claims that it was defectively manufactured and asks the buyer to pay for repairs, since French law provides for a seller's liability up to 10 years from delivery. The seller responds that the machine has stopped operating because the buyer improperly maintained it, and that in any event the contractual warranty, including for latent defects, has expired and the seller must now pay for repairs.

The parties are preparing for an arbitration over this dispute. In one paragraph, explain the seller's best argument for establishing that the buyer must pay the costs of the repairs and that the seller is not bound by the 10-year period for claiming latent defects.

Exercise 5.10: Basic

Assume the same situation as in Exercise 5.7, but in this case instead of providing for arbitration as a form of dispute resolution, the parties' contract specified that the courts at the buyer's principal place of business (Paris) would decide any disputes. The seller has initiated an 'expertise', a process by which the court appoints a technical expert (in this case, an engineer familiar with this type of equipment) to issue a report on which party is liable for the loss. It is known that French judges typically follow the recommendations contained in the reports of the experts they appoint. Do you think that in this situation, the French court will be more inclined to find the seller is bound by the 10-year latent defects period, or less? Explain in one paragraph.

Notes

Appendix
Guidelines to the Exercises

Chapter 1

Exercise 1.1

A. Dispute Forum
Some of the things that Amelie and Vishal would be well to consider are the following:
Areas of likely disputes: both parties should consider the most likely disputes that could arise under the SPA. A frequent source of disputes arising from M&A agreements is the seller's representations and warranties about the business at the time it was transferred, such as the accuracy of financial statements.
Enforceability: in the event that the acquiring company sues the Indian seller of the business in France, will the resulting court judgment be easily enforceable in India or any other country where an award debtor may have assets?
Language: considering the likely disputes to arise, will the French courts require the parties to pay for substantial translations of all supporting documents and have interpreters for witnesses and experts at any hearing? Given that English is likely to be the language of most documents (the assets are all in India) and the witnesses, the need to translate may impose considerable costs and delay.

B. Governing Law
While all three choices will be relevant in the contract negotiations, in Chapter 1 we make the case that the starting point of any inquiry about the choice of law or forum should always be (c), i.e. to understand the party's goals for entering into the contract and the problems that may arise. This will give the choice of law a purpose that is tied to the practical needs of the client when there is a future disagreement, the time when the chosen law will matter most.
The other considerations may be helpful but should not come after the client's actual needs.
Answer (a), choosing a law because it seems more familiar will make Vishal's boss happy and the acquiring company may find English or Singapore law more

acceptable. But these laws may not be as similar to Indian law as Vishal believes. Also, choosing a law because it seems more familiar may cause the lawyer to overlook any problems it might introduce. For example, will English law hold the seller to a strict interpretation of the representations and warranties in the contract and is this good for the seller? Or would the seller prefer a law that may incorporate notions of good faith in performance instead of a strict interpretation of the contract?

Answer (b) certainly *sounds* good. Who would want to propose the law of an 'unstable' and poorly regarded jurisdiction? In reality, the stability of a particular jurisdiction is important mainly when it is being proposed as a *forum* to resolve disputes. If it is not the forum selected by the parties, then the stability of a country may have no impact on its substantive laws.

Exercise 1.2

The inconvenience of a particular seat is generally not a problem because the arbitrators can always request that the hearings be held in a more easily accessible location. Moving the actual hearings (or holding them by telephone or video) does not change the contractually agreed seat of the arbitration.

The real risk is that judges in Grenoble are not likely to have the same level of experience dealing with international arbitration, or large international M&A disputes, than judges in a large city, like Paris.

Exercise 1.3

Vishal is right. The general rule is that any city may be the place of arbitration and there is no requirement that the parties or their contract have any connection with it. We explain that there are some rare exceptions to this, notably China, which may not permit enforcement of an award against a PRC mainland-based company unless it was held in the PRC under certain approved rules.

Exercise 1.4

Amelie is right. There is no requirement for the arbitration rules or the arbitration institution to have any connection with either the seat of the arbitration or the governing law. The ICC and the LCIA each publish statistics showing that for many of their cases, the seat of the arbitration, the governing law and the location of the parties have no connection with the cities in which each institution is headquartered (Paris and London).

Chapter 2

Exercise 2.1

Readers may be intuitively tempted to answer (a) and (c) as the laws of place of business of buyer and seller, respectively. The type of dispute that arises, however, may lead a court to consider the place of delivery or the place of storage of the goods to be of relevance to the interpretation of the contract performance.

GUIDELINES TO THE EXERCISES

Exercise 2.2
As a judge, you will be guided by the rules of private international law of your domestic law, in this case the Indonesian law. As discussed earlier in this chapter, the task of determining the applicable law by the judge will require undertaking a 'qualification' of the legal relationship and then identifying the 'connection' to a given legal system. Best practice would recommend that the Indonesian judge proceed to determine the applicable law on the basis of the guiding principles (e.g. *lex fori, lex loci celebrationis rule, locus regit actum, lex causae, lex loci protectionis*, etc.) which form the basis of Indonesian law.

Exercise 2.3
As the Saudi judge, you will need to consult your own legal system to search for answers including the rules that govern enforcement of foreign judgments and the guiding principles that would allow or refuse enforcement and the basis upon which a party might or might not prevail in its attempt to resist the enforcement of a foreign judgment.

Exercise 2.4
The Saudi judge may or may not apply Saudi law to this contract, and this decision will be guided by the rules of private international law of Saudi law. Parties might raise different arguments in an attempt to apply a different law on the basis of the contract circumstances (place of signature, place of performance, the law most closely connected, etc.); however, this will ultimately be determined by the rules of Saudi law.

Exercise 2.5
(i) In this case, the courts of Bahrain would in principle retain jurisdiction unless the civil procedure rules of Bahrain law provide otherwise or do not uphold the parties' negotiated clause.
(ii) According to the exercise, the goods are stored in the seller's warehouse in Dili (East Timor). From there the goods would be shipped be to the port of Al Jasra (Bahrain) where the buyer maintains a warehouse and a number of other businesses. Subject to other considerations regarding the contract provisions and prior agreement between the parties, the arbitrators might therefore conclude that the law most closely connected with the contract performance is Bahrain law.
(iii) In the absence of a clause designating a forum for resolving disputes, parties might run the risk of 'racing to the courthouse' and thus facing parallel (lengthy and expensive) court proceedings and contradictory court decisions.

GUIDELINES TO THE EXERCISES

Exercises 2.6 to 2.10

Negotiation: Preliminary Issues
Best practice dictates that understanding the full (legal) picture is the starting point to be fully acquainted with the available options. Some preliminary legal questions for reflection could be as follows:
i.   Would it be better for your client to have an agreed substantive law, even one that is that of the other party to the Contract (with which your client is not very familiar), instead of the uncertainty of leaving the applicable law open to be determined later by a judge?
ii. Are there any bilateral or multilateral agreement regarding matters of contractual obligations between these two jurisdictions?
iii. Are there international judicial cooperation agreements between these two jurisdictions?
iv. Are there unified conflict of law rules in the matter of contractual obligations?
v.   Would the courts of Hanoi accept the parties' choice of law or impose their own choice of law rules?
vi. The attitude of the Hanoi courts to contracts and the interaction with statute and mandatory provisions.
vii. What are the choice of law rules under Vietnamese law?
viii. What is the Vietnamese's legal tradition?

Factors to Consider in the Choice of the Governing Contract Law
Once you have taken steps with a view to minimizing the potential dangers set out above, you may wish to lay down some 'hard-and-fast' rules and consider other issues:
i.   What protection/remedy is most likely to be needed given the asset being sold, the industry sector and my client's position in the contract?
ii. What law provides that protection/remedy?
iii. Is a literal interpretation of the contract commended or expected?
iv. Is a contextual evaluation of the relationship commended or expected?
v.   'Home turf' – is it wise in the circumstances to avoid the other party's law?
vi. Are the laws being considered particularly developed in that area and sufficiently accessible?
vii. What is the contract theory followed and how much freedom to contract is allowed by the law?

Application of the CISG
As discussed in Chapter 2, the application of the CISG may occur independently (Art. 1(1)(a)) or by rules of private international law (Art. 1(1)(b)). The independent or direct application occurs when the contracting parties are located in states that have ratified the CISG. The application of the CISG via rules of private international law occurs when the judge, while searching for the applicable law, concludes that it is the law of a contracting state. It seems therefore clear and

intuitive that, in such a case, the law of the contract will be the CISG since, upon ratification, this legal framework joined the legal system of the state.

It is also important to remember that the CISG may be a standalone choice in an agreement subject to arbitration. To err on the side of caution, it is advisable to confirm that the arbitration acts or regulations concerned allow for such choices. In a contract not subject to arbitration, i.e. a judicial court clause, it will be necessary to understand whether the courts that will adjudicate the agreement support a choice of law clause or will impose their own choice of law rules.

Reservations to the Application of the CISG
As we have also discussed in Chapter 2, it is important to remember that there are exceptions that may curtail the application of the CISG even if both parties are located in contracting states. Exceptions are provided for in Articles 90, 92, 93 and 94. Article 90 deals with the case of international agreement (concluded or that may be) between the states concerned and which relates to provisions on matters governed by the CISG. In such a case, the CISG will not apply. Article 92 allows states to make reservations regarding Part I and Part II of the CISG. Article 93 provides for the cases where a contracting state has two or more territorial units. Article 94 authorizes contracting states that contain identical or similar legal rules on matters governed by the CISG to declare its inapplicability. Finally, domestic laws may apply in some cases to supplement the matters uncovered by the CISG via Article 7(2).

Caution should be exercised here as regards the act of ratification of the CISG and not the act of signature. Ratification involves the completion of internal legal and administrative procedures of each state for the instrument to be incorporated into domestic law thereby generating legal effects. For this reason, the CISG provides in Article 100 that the instrument applies to contracts concluded from the date of entry into force of the CISG.

Exercise 2.11
On the assumption that the parties have agreed to an arbitration clause with Singapore as the seat, the eye-catching factors should be (c), (d) and (f). Factor (a) is not really relevant at all, as long as the country's laws and courts will recognize the validity of an agreement to arbitrate. Factor (b) may be relevant to the substantive issues if a dispute arises between the parties over an alleged violation of environmental laws by one of them, in which case may also be relevant to the arbitration award rendered, but it is not relevant to the enforceability of an arbitration agreement. Factor (e) is not relevant for the purpose of this exercise because the parties have already agreed to Singapore being the seat of the arbitration.

Exercise 2.12
Much of what has been discussed in Guidelines Exercises 2.6 to 2.10 will be relevant in Exercise 2.12 also. However, in this case the parties wish to have a 'comprehensive legal framework to bind future agreements'. This gives rise to a number of other issues that may have to be considered, such as:
– What is the attitude of the courts in Switzerland and Hong Kong towards this type of contractual arrangement?
– Would this legal framework be valid and enforceable under Swiss law and the law of Hong Kong?
– What would be the gap fillers in case of matters not covered by this legal framework?
– What are the dispute resolution options on the card? How would the dispute resolution options intertwine with the choice of law?
– As regards dispute resolution matters, consider various and complex court procedures; litigation and arbitration costs; contract type; technical and specialized nature of the potential dispute; the nature and longevity of the collaboration sought; and enforcement concerns.

Exercise 2.13
Remember that you are asked to elaborate a skeleton of the legal framework that will bind the parties going forward and not a full-blown framework. We suggest that you prepare a timeline of a contractual relationship and fill in each phase chronologically.

Drafting the Principles

General Provisions
– Definitions
– Freedom of contract
– Freedom of form
– Good faith (usages and practices)
– Mandatory rules

Contract Formation
– Offer and acceptance
– Time of acceptance
– Late acceptance
– Modifications – amendments

Validity
– Grounds for avoidance (fraud, error, etc.)

Contract Interpretation
– Intention of the parties

- Conduct of the parties
- Relevant circumstances

Contract Performance
- Time of performance
- Place of performance
- Payment (by) means
- Currency
- Hardship

Non-performance
- Force majeure
- Termination (notice – right to terminate)
- Damages
- Gap fillers

Exercise 2.14
It makes economic sense to commence this exercise with questioning the viability of using this legal framework:
- Can the parties use this set of principles?
- If so, can the parties use them in court proceedings? Will the courts accept and apply this set of principles?
- Can the parties use this set of principles in arbitration proceedings? Will the applicable Arbitration Act or Regulation allow such choice and the Arbitral Tribunal abide by the parties' choice?
- What are the other alternatives available? Are the parties bound by any other convention or treaty, bilateral or otherwise, unified conflict of law rules in the matter of contractual obligations? Are a-national rules recognized as law or principles of law under the jurisdiction where the parties might seek enforcement of the award or court decision?
- If the answers to the above were satisfactory, it would also be recommended to understand the following:
- Would this legal framework cover sale of goods only?
- Would parties intend to have a well-rounded legal framework?
- Would parties be agreeable to use other sources of law?

Exercise 2.15
You need to take into account all matters that might be of relevance in this negotiation and have clear avenues and exit routes tied to its purposes. There is also an economic component to be factored into this equation, which is the commercialization of the asset. Much of what has been discussed in the guidelines above will be relevant in this case as well. We would suggest considering what might amount to a key points action plan and outlining it in bullet point format:

GUIDELINES TO THE EXERCISES

- What protection/remedy is most likely to be needed given the asset being traded, the industry sector and my client's position in the contract?
- What law provides that protection/remedy?
- Is a literal interpretation of the contract commended or expected?
- Is a contextual evaluation of the relationship commended or expected?
- 'Home turf' – is it wise in the circumstances to avoid the other party's law?
- Are the laws being considered (especially IP) particularly developed in that area (biotechnology, bioethics) and sufficiently accessible?
- What is the contract theory followed and how much freedom to contract is allowed by the law?
- What are the dispute resolution options on the card? How would the dispute resolution options intertwine with the choice of law? What courts and traditions (civil or common law) are being considered? Will the courts accept the parties' choice of law or impose their own choice of law rules?
- The attitude of the courts to the contract and the interaction with statute and mandatory provisions;
- As regards dispute resolution matters, consider various and complex court procedures; litigation and arbitration costs; contract type; technical and specialized nature of the potential dispute; short product cycle; the nature and longevity of the collaboration sought and enforcement concerns.

Potential Breaches of Contract by Buyer and Seller
It is a rather Herculean task to predict how parties would behave in the course of a contract performance. However, given the industry sector, the subject matter and the types of agreements generally used in this field, some words of warning would assist you to be fully acquainted with the potential risks often seen and be able to gain the upper hand.

Buyer and Seller – Contract Negotiations
The prudent course would be, firstly, to enquire whether the buyer already holds patents for the protection of the protein and, if so, in which jurisdictions. If not, the buyer should conduct a thorough research and analysis as to whether this protein could be patentable and, if so, the (including geographic) scope of protection sought for patents (for example, the Patent Cooperation Treaty should be taken into account, especially as the United States and European Union are both part of this treaty for international patent protection). In conjunction with the patent protection, the buyer should look into protecting its intangible asset through a wider range of intellectual property regimes, such as trademarks, designs and even rights obtained under plant breeder rights. As the buyer, you should also bear in mind that unregistered rights may be recognized in some EU jurisdictions (e.g. the United Kingdom) as a passing off right.
- Once the buyer has had some clarity regarding the patentability of the protein and other forms of IP protection, it would be sensible to turn to the commercialization aspect of the asset. To this end, the parties will need to

consider the type of agreement required: perhaps a Secrecy Agreement and a further Development, License and Supply Agreement. If so, in light of the sensitivities and the potential monetary value revolving around this matter, the parties should also consider including an arbitration clause in the agreement. The parties should also consider confidentiality provisions. For a discussion about the peculiarities of the arbitration clause, we should refer you back to the first paragraph of the guidelines to Exercise 2.9.
- The parties should also clearly define each party's rights and obligations under the agreement: for example, the buyer will manufacture and supply the protein whereas the seller will develop the products in compliance with clinical tests; would the product be sold in the field under the buyer's own trademark? What is the agreed lump sum and any other payments required under the agreement?
- It is more likely that the buyer would grant the seller an exclusive license for the patents to manufacture, use and sell the products. The license might or might not include the right to sublicense.

Potential Breaches
- Patent infringement
- Trademark infringement
- Breach of confidentiality provisions under the Agreement
- Breach of the Agreement for reasons of costs of performance; default in payment from any of the parties

Exercise 2.16
On the assumption that the dispute will be decided by arbitration, there might be less hurdles in implementing this 'dépeçage law' in comparison to court cases, but let us not forget to err on the side of caution and ensure that the arbitration acts or regulations concerned allow for such 'mosaic' choices. In addition, the arbitrators will have to be well aware of this arrangement and is commendable that this be raised by the arbitrators in a Procedural Order in early stages of the proceedings to ensure that such arrangement effectively reflects the present intention of the parties. It is often the case that a contract is negotiated under very different circumstances from the ones in which a dispute arises. There is another layer of complexity to be considered here, which is the operability of the clause given potential conflicting provisions.

Exercise 2.17
The choice of law clause could read as follows:
The domestic laws of California, without regard to any conflict of law rules, shall govern this Agreement. The United Nations Convention on Contracts for the International Sale of Goods (CISG) shall not govern this Agreement, the application of which is expressly excluded save for its Part II (Formation of the Contract, Arts. 14-28).

GUIDELINES TO THE EXERCISES

Chapter 3

Exercise 3.1

As we have discussed above, the absence of a contractual choice of forum can potentially point to different jurisdictions when a dispute arises under an international commercial contract. However, in general terms, a party may always be sued in the place where it has its registered office or where it undertakes its main business, and even at the place where the main performance was to be carried out. But it would be a good practice to understand the available options fully. Some preliminary thoughts for reflection could be as follows:

– Potential advantages or disadvantages of the rules of civil procedure and of evidence, or limitations that might make proving the claim or a defence to a claim more difficult. For example, what is the contract obligation that will be alleged to have been breached? Is this something that would make it useful to obtain internal documents from the other side, such as the process of ensuring that personnel have the correct training and qualifications for their positions? If so, then perhaps a jurisdiction that permits liberal 'discovery' of documents from the other side, New York or Miami, would be more advantageous than civil law jurisdictions like Mexico and Brazil, where this opportunity will be more limited.
– The party's familiarity with the courts in a particular legal system is certainly a reasonable factor that a party will want to consider, so long as it is not the only consideration.
– Language: this is not just a question for a preference for the language to be used in the proceeding, which could make the dispute easier or more difficult for the party to conduct and/or supervise. If the language of most of the documentary evidence and witnesses will need to be translated in order to be understood by the judge (or comply with rules or court practice), this could add substantial costs and delays.
– The court's reputation for neutrality, efficiency and the quality of its decisions.
– The most important factor for a claimant will nearly always be the ability to enforce a judgment, whether in the same country or in a different one, from the courts if that is where the other party's assets are located.

Variation 1: If the defendant has assets only in Mexico, then clearly the easiest way to enforce against its assets would be a judgment of a court in Mexico. But the party should still consider whether other factors, such as the rules of evidence or even the neutrality of the courts, make it unlikely that a claim against a Mexican defendant would succeed. If the conclusion is that the party would not win in the home jurisdiction of the defendant and that this is the only location where the defendant has any assets, then it should question whether the claim should be brought at all. This is true with regard to bringing claims in the courts of any country.

Variation 2: If the contract contains an arbitration clause, the party should initiate arbitration proceedings in accordance with such clause. The components of an arbitration clause, including its extension and scope, are discussed in Chapters 3 and 4 and should be taken into account in the present analysis. In addition, it is worth noting that New York Convention will give the resulting arbitration award the legal effect of a judgment of the course of first instance in the country of enforcement, which is any of the 166 states that have ratified it.

Exercise 3.2: Basic
Since the parties have specified Latvian courts in their contract, a Latvian court will likely find that it has jurisdiction over the dispute against a defendant in Germany, especially since one of the parties is a Latvian national.

Further, both Latvia and Germany are contracting states of the Hague Convention on Choice of Court, concluded in 2005 and which came into force on 1 October 2015. This is another reason for the courts of either Latvia or Germany a to hear any dispute arising out their contract.

Exercise 3.3: Intermediate
The parties have elected the courts of Portugal to hear any contractual dispute. If a dispute arises, the Hague Convention will apply to the agreement and will require the Portuguese court to take jurisdiction. Nevertheless, unless and until Brazil becomes a contracting state, the Hague Convention will not prevent a Brazilian court from taking jurisdiction nor will it require it to enforce a judgment of the Portuguese court.

What might also amount to a key action is the fact that the seller (Brazilian party) has assets in Angola and Mozambique. If the Portuguese party obtains a favourable ruling before the Portuguese court, it may wish to try its luck and enforce the judgment in these African countries on the basis of the Agreements of Legal and Judicial Cooperation between Portugal and these countries.

Lastly, let us not forget that if the country where the Portuguese party seeks enforcement has not acceded to the Hague Convention at the time of the enforcement, domestic law will apply to determine whether the judgment can be enforced.

Exercise 3.4: Basic
a. Since the claim would be based on a contract for optimizing searches in English-speaking countries, and the work is being performed in Canada, a large portion of the documentation is likely to be in English. This could impose very substantial costs on both parties for translating claim documentation into Chinese.
b. The Chinese party should not assume that a judgment rendered in the PRC will be easily enforceable in Canada, if that is where the Canadian seller has its assets. In the absence of any treaties for recognizing and enforcing foreign judgments, Canadian courts may be reluctant to enforce the Chinese court

judgment. If the Canadian party has no assets in China, the Chinese party may wish to insist on a form of financial guaranty (such as a letter of credit), which may increase the cost of contracting for the seller (and the price of the contract for the buyer). Alternatively, the Chinese party may wish to consider arbitration or the courts of Canada.

c. The contract and any potential dispute would appear to involve very technical issues. If the judge does not have sufficient technical expertise to understand the disputed issues, this may go against either or both parties in their efforts to prove their case.

d. Obviously, it would be more expensive for the Canadian seller to send witnesses to China to participate in hearings and preparation.

Variation: More suitable for open discussion. If the Chinese company is most concerned about being able to enforce a right to reimbursement if the Canadian company does not deliver the work according to the contract, then it should consider specifying arbitration instead of the courts.

Exercise 3.5: Basic
Tunis, because the goods would be there and that is the location to apply to the courts for interim relief.

Variation 1: If the goods are in United Kingdom, then the English courts would have jurisdiction over them.

Variation 2: If the buyer wishes to sue the seller for damages, its home location – Chad – is the option the buyer should assess.

Exercise 3.6: Intermediate
It would make sense as a practical matter to initiate court proceedings in Singapore as it is the buyer's place of business, in order to collect the sums owed as quickly as possible.

Variation: The seller's best course of action would be to resist the action in the courts of Singapore, assuming it wishes the buyer to take delivery of the goods. Of course, since the buyer is defaulting, the seller may not want this result and may instead accept not to deliver goods to a defaulting buyer and instead ask the Singapore court to order the buyer to comply with its existing payment obligations and award all other breach of contract damages.

Exercise 3.7: Intermediate
All of these factors are relevant in the abstract and prior to a dispute. The absence of a contractual choice of forum can potentially point to different jurisdictions when a dispute arises under an international commercial contract. However, in general terms, a party may always be sued in the place where it has its registered

office or where it undertakes its main business (factor 5) and even at the place where the main performance was to be carried out (factor 3).

On the assumption that the goods are in Sohar, you might need to initiate court proceedings in the courts of Sohar, being the place mostly connected with the contract (4). In doing so, factor (1) becomes relevant, as the underlying contract contains a choice of law clause according to which the laws of England and Wales apply. This will provide you with the legal framework with which to construe your case. If, however, there was no choice of law clause in the underlying contract, or if the choice of law clause was defective, factors (2)-(4) would assist in the determination of the applicable law. As it stands, these factors, including factor (5), could also be relevant in a prospective tort claim. Factor (5) is also relevant for the purpose of notification and service of the legal action, documents and enforcement reasons.

Exercise 3.8: Basic
The correct answer is (a). If a dispute arises, the Hague Convention will apply to the agreement and will require the Mexican court to take jurisdiction. However, unless and until Brazil becomes a contracting state, the Hague Convention will not prevent a Brazilian court from taking jurisdiction nor will it require the Brazilian courts to enforce a judgment rendered by a Mexican court.

Exercise 3.9: Advanced
a. The parties have elected the courts of Portugal to hear any contractual dispute. If a dispute arises, the Hague Convention will apply to the agreement and will require the Portuguese court to take jurisdiction. Nevertheless, unless and until Brazil becomes a contracting state, the Hague Convention will not prevent a Brazilian court from taking jurisdiction nor will it require it to enforce a judgment of the Portuguese court.

b. What might also amount to a key action is the fact that the seller (Brazilian party) has assets in Angola and Mozambique. If the Portuguese party obtains a favourable ruling before the Portuguese court, it may wish to try its luck and enforce the judgment in these African countries on the basis of the Agreements of Legal and Judicial Cooperation between Portugal and these countries.

Lastly, let us not forget that if the country where the Portuguese party seeks enforcement has not acceded to the Hague Convention at the time of the enforcement, domestic law will apply to determine whether the judgment can be enforced.

Exercise 3.10: Basic
a. The obvious risk that João's company faces, and probably the first thing his managers will ask, is the assurance of getting paid. As Astrid is proposing the contract, if her company defaults on payment after taking title to the goods, João's company will need to sue. Other possible risk areas are claims of defects/

GUIDELINES TO THE EXERCISES

warranty for the parts, but these are likely to be secondary to João's company if they are not paid for their work in the first place.
b. Among the things that João should consider are where a suit would need to be filed, in the courts of Brazil (seller's home and the place of delivery) or the courts of Poland, home of the buyer? If they sue in Brazil, would the courts accept jurisdiction over the Polish company, could the resulting judgment be easily enforced in Poland and how long might that take? If Poland, would this have to be in Elblag, a small town where Astrid's company will have a large economic presence? Will the Polish court accept jurisdiction in relation to the performance of a contract in Brazil?
c. If Astrid remains intractable on dispute resolution, one way to address the risk of non-payment is to insist on different terms elsewhere in the contract. In this case, João could propose that manufacturing will not begin for any parts unless they are paid in full in advance or there is a letter of credit or other financial guarantee in place.

Exercise 3.11: Basic
The better answer is (b). João can tell his boss – diplomatically – that limiting the scope of arbitrable disputes to certain situations may actually introduce more risk for their company. The original language is broad enough to cover claims that the contract was never valid, or even of fraud or wrongful termination. It is an open question whether a court would view the more specific language proposed by João's boss to cover a claim of fraudulent inducement to enter the contract or wrongful termination.

Exercise 3.12: Basic
Yes. The new language still includes the broad, general language, and it is clear that the ability to decide disputes relating to the contract formation are not the only ones the arbitrators may decide.

Exercise 3.13: Intermediate
The best solution to protect the company's technology is (b), to make sure that the parties remain free to go to court for an injunction or other urgent relief. Courts typically have this jurisdiction even if there is an arbitration agreement, but specifying this in the arbitration agreement will avoid any ambiguity as to what the parties intended.
Option (a) introduces new problems, in addition to abandoning the advantages of arbitration. Specifying the courts of Poland, for example, will be useful if it is expected that a violation of trade secrets will happen there, but what if the trade secrets are disclosed to a competitor in Hungary or South Korea? Will courts in those countries honour an injunction or urgent measure issued by a Polish court? Most likely the claimant will need to file a new claim in those courts, which is the same result provided in option (b).

Option (c) seems appealing on its face, but it introduces complexity that may be problematic. For example, if the dispute is whether the Polish company is breaching the agreement by disclosing proprietary technical information, should this be treated as a technical matter for the expert or a legal matter for the arbitrators? The answer may unfortunately be both, giving the claimant the option of choosing which forum to proceed in and the respondent an opportunity to contest jurisdiction no matter which forum is chosen. Clauses referring disputes to expert resolution are also troublesome because of the uncertain legal status of expert determination: is it arbitration or is it some other form of dispute resolution? Another difficult issue is whether the arbitrators will be able to reopen matters determined by an expert and, if so, in which circumstances?[84]

Exercise 3.14: Basic
Yes to both questions.
An arbitral institution is an organization that administers arbitrations, wherever they may be. The freedom to choose the place of arbitration is provided by the rules of most arbitral institutions. The location of an institution in a given city does not mean that the place of arbitration must also be in the same city, although that is frequently the case. Some institutions, like the ICC, the LCIA, SIAC and several others, administer the majority of their arbitrations in jurisdictions other than the one where they are headquartered.
Similarly, the legal seat of the arbitration typically does not impose an obligation for any physical activity, such as hearings or a tribunal's meetings to deliberate, to occur there. If the English party insists on London as the 'place of arbitration', Chiara could accept this on condition that 'any hearings will be conducted in Milan'.

Exercise 3.15: Intermediate
(b) The arbitrators can simply conduct the hearing in a country for which all arbitrators and counsel can gain entry without difficulty, generally identified and agreed after consulting the parties. The legal seat of the arbitration will still be Jeddah, and any challenge to the arbitrators' award will need to take place there, but the physical activities of the arbitration can take place somewhere else. Of course, instead of waiting for the arbitral institution (if any) to raise the matter with the parties, and the parties to agree subsequently, or the arbitrators (once appointed) to address the matter, the parties could also have specified the different legal seat and place of hearings in their arbitration agreement.

Exercise 3.16: Intermediate
Since Binghamton is a small city, the buyer may not be able to easily obtain adequate information on whether it has courts that are neutral or efficient. But a bigger issue for both parties may simply be that the judges in a small city are

---

84 McIlwrath & Savage, *supra* note 8, pp. 1-016.

unlikely to have experience with international arbitration and complex international commercial disputes. It is advisable for both parties to select a city with an international reputation as a seat of arbitration, such as New York, Miami or Houston in the United States. The courts of large cities like these will have experience in supporting the process of arbitration.

Exercise 3.17: Intermediate
With an institution, such as the ICC or the LCIA, the claimant must simply comply with the requirements for submitting the request for arbitration directly to the institution, which typically includes payment of a filing fee and compliance with the filing requirements under the rules, and the institution will then 'notify' the respondent of the commencement of proceedings and of the time limits for responding to the request. In contrast, in an *ad hoc* proceeding, the parties would have agreed to the governing rules previously (e.g. UNCITRAL Arbitration Rules), including the notification and commencement of the arbitration proceedings. There is a third option, a sort of hybrid, in which the parties agree that an arbitration institution will act as administering authority in an *ad hoc* arbitration, such as confirming the appointment of the arbitrators and dealing with any challenges, requesting fees on behalf of the arbitrators and paying them, and offering both the arbitrators and the parties all the necessary administrative support for the efficient conduct of the arbitration. There is also a fourth option, which is similar to the third option, but in this case the arbitration institution acts as appointing authority only. In other words, the role of the institution is not to provide administrative support throughout the entirety of the case but rather ceases as soon as the arbitration institution appoints the arbitrators.

Exercise 3.18: Advanced
All of the elements could benefit from being more specific. Factor (a) negotiation of senior executives should provide more elements on how would this process be carried out, who are the 'senior executives', how long it should last and when the negotiation period would be deemed to have terminated so there is no unfulfilled condition to starting an arbitration. Factor (b) could identify which of the three different sets of UNCITRAL Arbitration Rules available, i.e. 1976, 2010 and 2013. And factor (c), 180 days to complete the arbitration could be problematic since it does not define when the arbitration starts (from the notice of arbitration or the constitution of the arbitral tribunal) and when it ends (at the close of the hearing or upon the issuance of the final award).
Additionally, the clause does not mention the place of arbitration, and the parties may well want to consider specifying this.

Exercise 3.19: Basic
1. Concerns and Risks
Concerns
- Goodwill: the Institution is unheard of in the marketplace; it is unclear as to whether (and how) the institution operates in practice.
- Transparency: the Institution has no website publicly available, no easily accessible set of arbitration rules and no guidelines regarding the arbitration process or general information about the services provided, fees, physical address, members of the Secretariat, etc.;
- Due process: the rules are not available and the process of appointment of arbitrators is rather unclear. The words of the President of the Institution are particularly worrisome, given that the process is based on 'friendships' and that counsel, whom the President of the institution knows, recommends the arbitrators.

Risks
- Fees and costs: unclear how much the arbitration service would cost in total; how to make interim payments in the course of the arbitration and whether the institution has mechanisms to hold funds legitimately for its clients or indeed hold funds at all?
- Due process: risk of being abided by unclear, unfair and unilateral rules.
- Quality of the decision: would any resulting arbitral award be of the standard expected, e.g. well-reasoned and ascertainable?
- Enforcement: would any resulting arbitral award be in compliance with the rules and laws applicable and enforceable?
- Criminal liability: if the institution is being run as an illegal operation, the client could be found liable for contributing to possible criminal activities (e.g. money laundering, etc.).

2. Talking Points

Legal Issues	Commercial Issues	Criminal Issues
Poorly reasoned award	Fees and costs	Irregular activity
Unenforceable award	Increased costs (court proceedings)	Institution with no legal personality
Fundholding	Risk of dissipation of funds	Money laundering
Fraud or any procedural illegality	Reputational damage, costs of opportunity	Sham arbitration and client found liable for contributing to illegal activity

Legal Issues	Commercial Issues	Criminal Issues
Professional negligence by legal representative	Costs (court proceedings)	Legal representative found liable for assisting and abetting illegal activity

Proposals
The buyer's proposed institution is a 'no go'. You should instead propose a reputable institution which would match the following criteria:
- **Credibility:** an institution respected in the marketplace, with a clear track record of commercial arbitration experience.
- **Transparency:** arbitration rules clearly ascertainable, from beginning to end of the proceedings, including transparency with respect to the appointment of arbitrators, costs, the handling of funds and the overriding respect for the due process and fair treatment.
- **Ethics:** a commitment to high ethical standards and appropriate mechanisms to enforce breaches in the course of an arbitration.
- **Expertise:** if the case requires certain expertise, you may wish to suggest an institution that is widely used by a particular industry sector, such as for insurance or maritime disputes, etc.

Exercise 3.20: Basic
(a)

Exercise 3.21: Intermediate
On the assumption that the parties have agreed to an arbitration clause, the eye-catching factors should be (3) and (5)-(6). Factor (1) is not really relevant at all, so long as the country's laws and courts will recognize the validity of an agreement to arbitrate (see factor 6). Factor (2) may be relevant to the substantive issues if a dispute arises between the parties over an alleged violation of environmental laws by one of them, in which case may also be relevant to the arbitration award rendered, but it is not relevant to the enforceability of an arbitration agreement. Factor (4) is not relevant, since international arbitration institutions need not be located in the same country as the seat of the arbitration. In contrast items 3, 5 and 6 all relate to the enforcement of agreements to arbitrate and also the enforceability of an international arbitration award.

Group Exercise 3.22: Intermediate
Discussion question: the parties have asked you to explain to them how you believe a tribunal in an international arbitration might approach their contractual choice of law differently from a judge. In discussing this in small groups, consider the education, training and experiences that a judge would have in applying a foreign law vs. an arbitrator who has sat in cases in which different laws have applied and how this might affect their receptivity to different legal arguments being advanced by the parties under the contract's choice of law.

GUIDELINES TO THE EXERCISES

Exercise 3.23
(e)

Exercise 3.24: Basic
The most problematic course of action would be to undertake option **(b)** given that the arbitration would be seated in Tripoli, which is situated in a jurisdiction not party to the 1958 New York Convention. The other options would need to be carefully considered on the basis of expertise required to adjudicate the dispute, arbitration costs and convenience for enforcement purposes as well.

Exercise 3.25: Intermediate
If the arbitration is to be seated in Africa, the parties should consider arbitral institutions and their experience in handling arbitrations in the region (and at the seat), and counsel and arbitrators familiar with the relevant courts.

Exercise 3.26: Intermediate
N'Djamena is situated in a jurisdiction not party to the 1958 New York Convention. Even if Chad is not a contracting state, the seller might have assets in Sudan, Mali and Somalia. Out of these jurisdictions, Sudan and Mali are contracting states, so a favourable arbitral award could be enforced against the seller in these jurisdictions under the 1958 New York Convention. You should not rule out the possibility of attempting to enforce the arbitral award in the courts of N'Djamena, since the arbitration award will be a 'local' one, not requiring recognition of a foreign award. In addition, parties should investigate whether there are any conventions or treaties for legal integration and judicial cooperation which might assist in the enforcement of arbitral awards in any other jurisdiction (e.g. OHADA).

Exercise 3.27: Basic
Mediation is a proven method for facilitating settlement. As noted in this section, requiring mediation before arbitration can help reduce the perceived risk of arbitrating in a difficult jurisdiction by increasing the likelihood of settling. Alexis might also propose institutional arbitration, instead of *ad hoc*, with a respected global institution like the ICC, the LCIA or SIAC, each of which has its own 'court' which, under each institution's rules of arbitration, will take the place of the courts at the seat with respect to all actions regarding the appointment of arbitrators. Further, Alexis could propose that while Port Harcourt would remain the seat, any hearings or meetings between the tribunal and the parties should occur in a different location.

Exercise 3.28: Intermediate
(b). It makes sense financially to initiate court proceedings in Singapore as the buyer's place of business.

GUIDELINES TO THE EXERCISES

Exercise 3.29: Intermediate
(b). For the same reasons, the seller's best course of action would be to resist the action in the courts of Singapore, assuming it wishes the buyer to take delivery of the goods. Of course, since the buyer is defaulting, the seller may not want this result and may instead accept not to deliver goods to a defaulting buyer and instead ask the Singapore court to order the buyer to comply with its existing payment obligations and award all other breach of contract damages.

Exercise 3.30: Basic
(a). Courts of Rotterdam as the choice of court agreed by the parties. Also, the seller would in any event be better off suing the defaulting party at its place of business.

Exercise 3.31: Basic
(b). Courts of Rotterdam as the choice of court agreed by the parties. A non-breaching party may be tempted to sue the defaulting party (in this case the Costa Rican seller) at its place of business. If the seller objects to lack of jurisdiction based on the contractual choice of court, however, the courts in San José might well dismiss the claim.

Chapter 4

Exercise 4.1: Basic
a. As noted, the LCIA does not have a 1996 set of rules. It has three sets of rules: 1998, 2014 and 2020. But this is generally not a serious problem. In this case, it is likely that the LCIA, in consultation with the parties, would determine which set of rules the parties meant to apply. This is only a problem if there are one or more provisions in the 1998, 2014 or 2020 rules that one of the parties wished to apply (or not have applied), in which case the matter might become more contentious and could require the Arbitral Tribunal, once appointed, to determine.
b. Paris: a reviewing court in Paris would likely conclude that the parties intended Paris as the legal seat or place of the arbitration, but certainly the parties could have been clear when expressing it, especially since the rest of the clause refers to the courts of a different country!
c. The clause creates the famous "race to the courthouse" by not excluding the jurisdiction of the courts in favour of arbitration. Most likely, whoever files first – in court or arbitration – may succeed in keeping the case there, with the risk that the result will be challenged later for having been decided in the wrong forum.
d. "Any dispute arising under or relating to this Agreement." This language is fine. It is broad and should encompass all disputes regarding the parties' contractual relationship.

Exercise 4.2: Advanced
The breadth of this choice of law is effectively no choice at all. The LCIA Rules expressly permit arbitrators to determine the applicable law to a contract. In this case, they would most likely look to the choice of law principles at the seat of the arbitration and may consider the nationality of the parties, the object of their contract and any relevant conventions or treaties such as the CISG.

Exercise 4.3: Intermediate
a. First and foremost, trade rules are not a 'law' but practices that may supplement one. The arbitrators would still need to determine which law should be applied to the parties' agreement, if only to determine its validity or the validity of any key terms. Once they have done this, they may look to trade associations (wine growers, winemakers, etc.) to determine if any provides for particular guidance on how contracts are typically entered into and enforced or if there are any standard terms that may be useful.
b. The opt in to the CISG would be of particular relevance here. For instance, Article 8 (3) of the CISG provides as follows "in determining the intent of a party or the understanding of a reasonable person would have had, due consideration is to be given to all relevant circumstances of the case including the negotiations, any practices which the parties have establishes between themselves, usages and any subsequent conduct of the parties". In addition, Article 9 of the CISG provides that the parties are bound by any use or practice established or agreed by them, as well as trade usages applicable to the contract and its formation, which is recognized in international trade and which (unless otherwise agreed by the parties) the parties knew or ought to have known. This would have captured the parties' intentions. Another option, equally relevant, would be the UNIDROIT Principles (e.g. Art. 1.9 (usages and practices)), "the parties are bound by a usage that is widely known to and regularly observed in international trade by parties in the particular trade concerned expect where the application of such a usage would be unreasonable". Lastly, and alternatively, the parties could agree to the laws of Alberta, France or a third country.
c. "Rules and principles applicable to the international wine industry" are vague. Subject to (b) above, if the parties could come to an agreement as to a set of standard provision adopted by an institutional body (if any), that would provide legal certainty.

Exercise 4.4
The choice of law clause has no material elements pointing to any particular law. You should therefore advise against such wording as this could pose a real threat to your client's interests if the case goes to arbitration. In addition, if an arbitration is initiated, it is important to remember that arbitrators are not bound by any rules of private international law and arbitration rules often allow arbitrators to determine the law applicable to an agreement on the basis of certain criteria, such as the

nationality of the parties, the place of performance, place of execution of the agreement, the seat of the arbitration, etc.

Variation:
a) No such laws really exist. The ICC is an arbitral institution. Therefore, the consequence of this option is that no choice of law has actually been agreed by the parties. If such clause is adopted, the parties will be asked by the arbitrator(s) to provide clarification (and possibly submissions) as a preliminary matter in the proceedings. However, it looks as though the Turkish party would be willing to choose an institutional arbitration rather than an *ad hoc*, and the Spanish party should explore this possibility and weigh in the pros and cons as discussed in Chapter 4.
b) There is an alternative here between Spain and Turkey, which is rather confusing. As in a) above, if this clause is adopted, the parties will be asked by the arbitrator(s) to provide clarification (and possibly submissions) as a preliminary matter in the proceedings. Another point of practice to note is that the parties have expressly included that the law will govern questions regarding the 'subject matter', 'validity' and 'enforcement'. Nonetheless, the parties have – deliberately or not – left out questions such as the 'existence', 'interpretation', 'formation', 'performance', 'breach', 'termination' of the Agreement – would they be agreeable to a *dépeçage* of laws for each of these categories? That would be highly undesirable. Subject to any particularities in the agreement, a reference to existence, validity or termination would generally be sufficient. In most of the cases, less is more!

Exercise 4.5

The reference to 'material law' is unclear, and so are the references to 'statutory' and 'common law'. The applicable law, as drafted, is rather confusing and convoluted. There is no such thing as 'the law of the United Kingdom'. There are, instead, the laws of England and Wales, or the laws of Scotland, etc. The main concern would therefore be whether an arbitrator appointed in the case would be able to determine the applicable law with sufficient predictability. In addition to the indeterminacy of the exact legal framework that would apply to the agreement, this uncertainty could also give the other side ammunition to challenge the enforceability of any resulting award.

Variation 1: The easiest way to do that would be to delete the references to 'material', 'statutory' and 'common law' and to refer to the laws of 'England and Wales'.

Variation 2: Both (a) and (b) are troublesome and require careful attention. First, what are the laws of the courts of the United Kingdom? There is no such law *per se*; however, it would suggest that the parties would perhaps like to consider the laws of England and Wales. Secondly, the reference to 'conflict of laws rules' is equally unhelpful because it does not have a starting point or a centre of gravity, i.e. laws of country X or Y.

Variation 3: There are various ways in which to draft such clause, for example: "the Agreement shall be governed by the laws of England and Wales, without regard to the principles of conflict of law rules of any jurisdiction" or "the Agreement shall be governed by the laws of Canada to the exclusion of any other law that may be imputed in accordance with choice of law rules applicable in any jurisdiction".

Exercise 4.6: Basic
a. To dispel any potential procedural irregularities, we should probably delete part [d] as there might be conflicting provisions between 'Brazilian Code of Civil Procedure' and the 'Civil Code of France', regarding the 'arbitration procedure', including how the law of the place of arbitration (Paris) would intertwine with the Brazilian law provisions in the designation of the arbitrations.
b. Potential issues to consider:
    – What is the meaning and the potential legal effects of the words 'arbitration procedure' in the clause;
    – Are there any conflicting provisions between 'Brazilian Code of Civil Procedure' and the 'Civil Code of France' regarding 'arbitration procedure' and
    – How the law of the place of arbitration (Paris) would intertwine with the Brazilian law provisions in the designation of the arbitrators.
    – Alternatives:
    – The safest way would be to attempt to contact the Chinese buyer to vary or amend the arbitration clause.
    – If no agreement is reached and a dispute eventually arises, you will be left out with the option to, once arbitration proceedings have begun, request the tribunal to address these questions as a preliminary matter.

Exercise 4.7: Basic
Much of what has been discussed in Chapter 3 and Guidelines to Chapter 3 Exercises apply here as well, with the additional issue of appointment of arbitrators. Parties might find themselves in a deadlock scenario if the co-arbitrators are unable to agree a Chair candidate. The default mechanism is rather truncated and there is a great deal of indeterminacy as to its mechanics.

The following examples are just some of the problems that might arise, and many other problems are certainly possible!
a. *The lack of an appointing authority*: Potential problem that could arise: Example: Party A refuses to propose a list of arbitrators for Party B to consider, and there is no reference to what authority should resolve this lack of action by Party A.

GUIDELINES TO THE EXERCISES

b. *The lack of agreed rules of arbitration*: Potential problem that could arise: The respondent disagrees that the claimant has validly notified its request for arbitration and refuses to participate in the arbitration or comply with the subsequent award. Depending on where enforcement is sought, the respondent may succeed in evading its debt arising from the arbitration award.
c. *The lack of a designated seat of the arbitration*: Potential problem that could arise: the respondent files a set-aside proceeding in an available country that is hostile to arbitration or files an opposition to the award in the courts at the place of enforcement, asking for a finding that the award is unenforceable under the rules of a different seat than the one declared by the arbitral tribunal. This delays or avoids enforcement of the arbitration award. If the parties had at least designated a seat of the arbitration, some of the other problems with this clause could have been mitigated.
d. *The reference to an 'Official List' from the ICC*: Potential problem that could arise: since the ICC has no such 'official list', the problem with this is self-evident. A party cannot propose names from a list that does not exist. There is no easy solution here, absent agreement with the opposing party. If the parties had designated an appointing authority, or at least a seat of arbitration (where an application to the courts could be made), this problem could have been avoided.

Exercise 4.8: Basic
Redrafting this as a valid ICC arbitration clause can be easily accomplished by simply referring to the ICC Rules of Arbitration in the place of the *ad hoc* mechanism, and specifying three arbitrations, which appears to be the parties' preference.
"Any disputes arising under this Agreement shall be finally resolved under the Rules of Arbitration of the International Chamber of Commerce (ICC) by three arbitrators appointed in accordance with the said Rules."

Exercises 4.9 and 4.10: Advanced
Exercises more suitable for open discussion.

Chapter 5

Exercise 5.1 Basic
Importance of relationship for considering issues of contract interpretation and disputes: Hopefully, each side will have considered not just the nature of the equipment being sold but the importance of the relationship between RQL and IM. Since the contract is likely to have warranty periods and limitations of liability in other provisions, the lawyers need not imagine the possibility that disputes will arise under the contract for the entirety of 20-30 years that the equipment is expected to be in operation. But they should expect the parties are likely to have a

commercial and technical relationship during this period and that their relationship may well be challenged by any disputes that arise.

One-sided vs. balanced dispute clauses: There are two generally opposing strategies for negotiating how a contract will handle any disputes that may arise. The first is the 'one-sided' view, which holds that a party should aim in negotiation for terms that are most favourable to its side, and unfavourable to the other. The rationale for the one-sided view is that it will encourage the other side to settle a dispute – or discourage them from embarking on an arbitration – if they believe the process is not favourable to their side.

The other side is the 'balanced' view, which is that the parties should each feel they are relatively equals in their ability to activity and succeed through the contract's dispute and choice of law provisions. The rationale for the balanced view is that a party that feels it cannot obtain a fair resolution of disputes through the contract may retaliate against the other party in other ways, mainly by ending any contracts or future commercial relationship.

In the present example, there may be reasons one side or the other will prefer to adopt a one-sided or balanced view.

Discussion: is the result achieved in the negotiation more one sided or balanced and what might this mean for future disputes (in terms of prevention) and/or the parties' commercial relationship?

Flexibility pays; rigidity costs

There is risk and then there are perceptions of risk. Each side will likely insist strongly on points where they perceive the risk to be very high. But the question must be asked: is the risk real or does it simply reflect the negotiator's lack of flexibility in the negotiation or lack of familiarity with a particular term?

Take, for example, the question of the contract's *choice of law*. This can raise interesting issues arising from the legal cultures of the parties. On the one hand, RQL is a state-owned company and operates only in Qatar. It may be subject to policies regarding state-owned companies, for example, that require special permissions to accept a law other than Qatari law. Further, its in-house lawyers are likely to be familiar with the laws in Qatar and the surrounding region. On the other hand, IM is a company that sells equipment around the world. Its in-house lawyers will likely be experienced negotiating contracts all around the world and may not view different laws as risky or problematic as lawyers for a state-owned company that do not share this international experience.

For each of the other terms negotiated in this exercise, discuss why the parties might diverge in their flexibility and rigidity and whether this was apparent in the negotiation.

Price Negotiation

Finally, discuss whether any concessions were made with respect to price. How much was conceded (increased or decreased) and what was received (or purchased)

for this concession? Now consider how IM's shareholders or Qatari's taxpayers would react if they were informed that IM or RQL had conceded $5 million in order to obtain a better choice of law provision (for example) in one of their equipment contracts.
Would they deem this to be a good use of company or taxpayer money? Or would they rather have a less ideal choice of law or arbitration clause?

Mediation, a process where interests can easily be aligned: The exercise provides opportunities for the parties to find commonality in things that may be important to both of them. Mediation is a good way to preserve their relationship over time, given that this contract is for the delivery of equipment that will last many years and which may lead to other contracts between them (such as the sale of spare parts or operation and maintenance contracts).

Duration of arbitration: The parties may well want to ensure that any arbitration does not exceed a certain period of time, but they should also consider that the drafting of this concept may be more challenging than simple agreement. When does the arbitration 'begin'? And when does it end? If the parties are going to press for limitations on the duration of the arbitration, they should give some thought as to how this can be objectively determined so as not to give rise to a dispute over the validity of the dispute resolution agreement.

Language: While a party may want to require that any arbitration be conducted in its native language, they should also give some thought as to whether this will detrimentally impact (a) the costs of the arbitration and (b) the range of arbitrators they can appoint. Logically, a contract for the supply of highly engineered equipment like this one will likely have many (or most) documents in English. Many of these documents will need to be translated if the arbitration is conducted in a language other than English. Similarly, many of the witnesses will likely be fluent in English and will need to have an interpreter present when they give testimony. Further, the parties will have wide access to virtually the entire pool of qualified international arbitrators if the arbitration is in English. This range will be substantially narrowed to the subset of arbitrators who speak another language that is specifically required by the contract. Remaining silent on the requirement is a simple and effective means of addressing situations in which it is difficult for one party to concede that the arbitration will be conducted in a particular language. The general rule is that the arbitrations are conducted in the language of the contract, unless otherwise specified.

Exercise 5.2: Advanced
The critical difference between English and Swiss law on the issue of penalties/liquidated damages is that under English law they operate as a cap on liability and under Swiss law they do not preclude a claimant from seeking to prove and recover

a greater amount of loss (or a respondent from seeking to prove the actual losses were less and the penalty should be reduced).

The problem here, of course, is that the clause in question was drafted for application under Swiss law and is not a good match for English law.

1. An English judge would likely have no difficulty applying English law to the clause and could find that the penalty is a valid expression of contractual liquidated damages. In that case, the total amount delay-induced losses for which the claimant can be liable is the amount of the liquidated damages, not more. The $3 million would therefore be excluded.
2. A Swiss judge, by contrast, might struggle to apply English law to a contract clause that seems to be a normal practice under Swiss law. While there is always the possibility that a Swiss judge would try divine how an English judge would approach the contract, it is also possible that the Swiss judge would instead regard the clause under the Swiss law interpretation on the grounds that this was the parties' intentions. In that case, the Swiss judge may well hold that Swiss Machines can recover both the 5% penalty and the additional $3 million.
3. An international arbitral tribunal would likely look to English law to determine how the clause would be treated, and in doing so agree with the English judge that the $3 million cannot be recovered. If the parties appoint arbitrators that hail from jurisdictions that treat contractual penalties in a way similar to Swiss law, however, they may be more sympathetic to an argument for the larger recovery from Swiss Machines.

Exercise 5.3: Intermediate
This argument is available under English law, i.e. that the specified amount of liquidated damages was not a 'genuine pre-estimate' of losses. Of course, it will be for the vendor to prove this, which may be difficult. Further, if the vendor prevails on this argument, the result is the invalidation of the liquidated damages clause. At that point, the delay is simply a material breach of contract for which there is no cap on liability. Swiss Machines would be able to recover all losses that it can prove were caused by the vendor's delay in delivery.

Exercise 5.4: Basic
(a). New York is a common law jurisdiction that derived its laws from England. The law will treat lost profits as 'indirect' or 'consequential' damages. By contrast, French law is a civil law jurisdiction and would treat lost profits as a form of direct loss.

Exercise 5.5: Basic
(d) All of the above. Although the contract purports to exclude 'indirect or consequential loss', a French court unfamiliar with these concepts may determine that all of these losses can be characterized as the direct result of breaching the contract.

GUIDELINES TO THE EXERCISES

Exercise 5.6: Intermediate
Since French law does not recognize the concept of 'indirect or consequential loss', the parties should specifically identify all the types of losses they intend to exclude from liability, i.e. exclusions for 'lost profits', 'additional costs incurred', etc. Although an international arbitral tribunal may try harder than a French court to understand what the parties intended, if they chose to apply French law, then it is reasonable to assume there is a risk they would agree with a French court that excluding 'indirect' damages does not have the same meaning as it would under New York or English law.

Exercise 5.7: Basic
Choosing French law and expressly excluding the application of the CISG will lead to the application of domestic French law and this provides 10-year period by which a buyer may claim the existence of latent defects, i.e. an implied warranty at law.

Exercise 5.8: Basic
Since the CISG applies automatically to contracts for the sale of goods between parties in different contracting states, it will apply whether specified (b) or not (a) in this contract. But a clause that specifically refers to a domestic sale of goods law will mean that the parties have agreed to apply that domestic law. The CISG may not be fully excluded in this case, but the domestic sale of goods law will take precedence over it.

Exercise 5.9: Basic
The seller's best shot would be to rely on the principle of party autonomy under French law to invoke the binding effect of the contractually agreed 4-year period for claiming latent defects, which should take precedence over the default 10-year rule under French law and be given full effect by the arbitrators. If the seller, however, is unable to present any evidence of such agreement, the matter would have to be referred and ultimately decided by the arbitrators, once appointed, and on the basis of French law as the contractually agreed applicable law.

Exercise 5.10: Basic
The French court will likely scrutinize the facts and evidence presented before them in order to determine whether the parties have indeed agreed to a 4-year period over the default rule and whether such agreement is valid under French law. It is rather difficult to predict whether the French court would be more inclined to rule in favour of the buyer (i.e. 10-year period rather than 4), but the French court might, amongst other factors, look at the issue of a potential unbalance of bargaining power to determine this matter.

About the Authors

Gustavo Moser is a legal counsel at the London Court of International Arbitration (LCIA) and a subject coordinator at the Swiss International Law School (SiLS). Dr Moser obtained his PhD in International Commercial Law from the University of Basel, Switzerland, and has been working for over fifteen years with matters pertaining to cross-border contracts and dispute resolution mechanisms in various legal roles worldwide.

Michael McIlwrath is Vice President - Litigation for Baker Hughes, a global technology company. Since 1999, he has represented his company in disputes world-wide, including work in negotiations, mediation, and arbitration. He is also chairman of the Governing Body for Dispute Resolution Services at the ICC.

The views expressed in this book are those of the authors and do not necessarily reflect the views of their employers or the organizations with which they are associated.